ASAHI

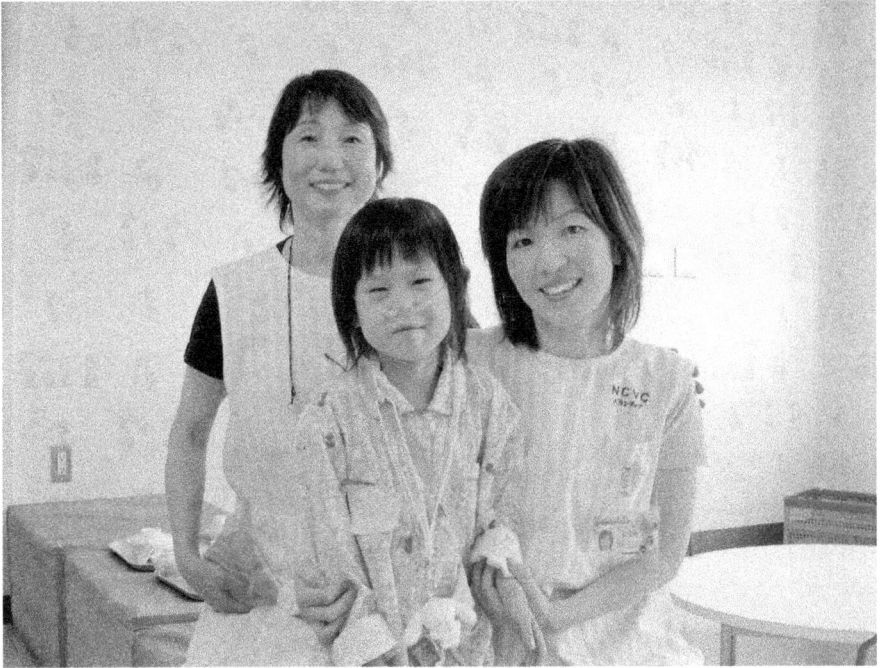

Asahi and Author with Ms. Mori (left)

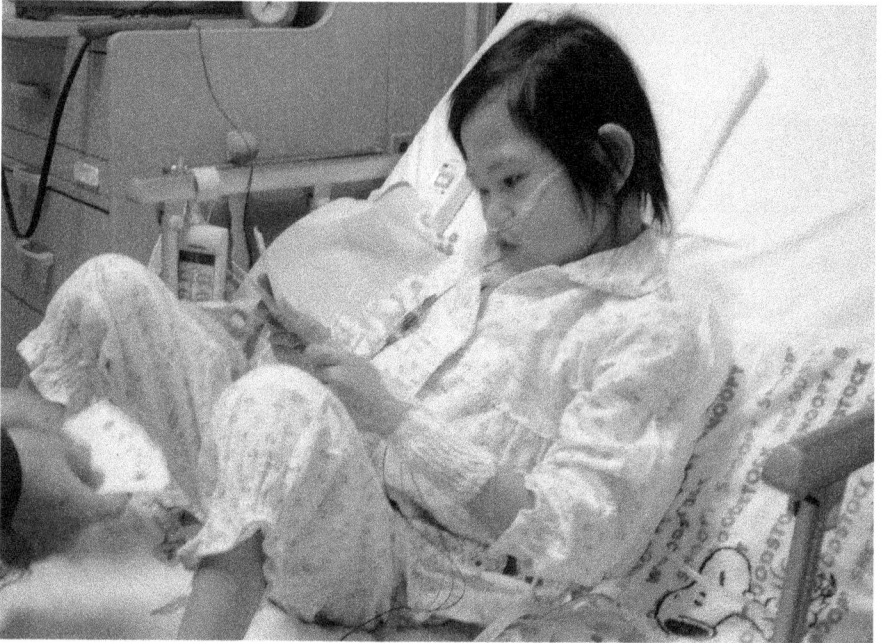

Asahi in the hospital

ASAHI
A MILLION THANK-YOUS

Taeko Maeda

Babel Press U.S.A.
Honolulu

ASAHI – A MILLION THANK-YOUS

Published by Babel Corporation.

This book was originally published in Japanese under the title
"朝陽　いっぱいのありがとう" by
Gentosha Renaissance, Tokyo, Japan in 2008.

Translation in English by Taeko Maeda
Supervision of translation by Hiroe Kobayashi
Stylish editing by Arnold Hiura

Cover design by Shingo Matsushima

Library of Congress Control Number: 2011910265
ISBN-13: 978-0983640202
ISBN-10: 0983640203

Babel Corporation
1110 University Avenue, Suite #510,
Honolulu, Hawaii 96826
Phone: (808) 946-3773
Fax: (808) 946-3993
Website: www.babel.edu

You know,
Parents think
They are watching their children,
But it is the children
Who are watching their parents
With even clearer eyes

—Mitsuo Aida

This book is dedicated to the girl who recognized with no doubt her mother's love, and to the mother who protected her daughter until the end.

Contents

ACKNOWLEDGMENTS

This English edition of *Asahi* could not have existed without Ms. Hiroe Kobayashi, my English teacher, who earnestly advised me to translate the original work and continued to constantly support and encourage me throughout the entire process. I have finally completed the whole work thanks to her.

Right after I published *Asahi* in Japanese, Ms. Kobayashi said to me, "I would recommend your book to my friends who can't read Japanese." Those words were amazingly full of enthusiasm. I owe her my deepest gratitude.

While I translated, she carefully corrected each word. Although she was very busy, she helped me translate this book purely out of goodwill. I mean that she did voluntary work on it for me.

I believe that Asahi would definitely say "thanks a million" to her. From now on, Asahi can have many friends who read the English version of her book.

When I started translating this book, Asahi's grandpa said to me, "If Asahi could have lived until she was twenty, I would have wanted to take her to the place where the novel *Anne of Green Gables* was set because it was my dream to bring her up like Anne."

Now I'm very glad that I can finally take "her" in the book to Prince Edward Island, Canada. I deeply appreciate that Ms. Hiroe Kobayashi could also realize Asahi's grandpa's dream because Asahi loved her grandpa very much.

With dreams that Asahi will be the Japanese Anne...

✤ ✤ ✤

I truly appreciate Mr. Yonezo Tsushi, who manages a bookstore named Loco Books. He is a friend of thirty years' standing, and he didn't spare himself.

If not for his knowledge and encouragement, I could not have written the original Japanese book. He kept pushing me to the very end, so I put my soul and heart into it. He didn't want me to leave out anything I felt towards Asahi so I wouldn't have any regrets. Thanks to his kindness, Asahi was born again as a book.

For the publication of this English version, Babel Corporation and its office manager and editor, Ms. Takae Okuma-Johnson who collaborated with a Honolulu-based writer and editor, Mr. Arnold Hiura did everything in their power. They consistently said to me, "We are fortunate to meet Asahi via your book and to publish it in English." I deeply appreciate that they could treasure Asahi's spirit and my book from start to finish.

PREFACE

On January 21, 2008, a nine-year-old girl passed away in Japan. Her name was Asahi, which means "the sun in the morning." True to her namesake, in life she was like the sun. During the five and a half years that I knew her, I saw many different sides of Asahi. But, now that she's gone, I can only remember her sun-like smile.

I wrote this book not to tell a story of how much a young girl had endured. Rather, I want to share with everyone what a joyful child Asahi was, how strong she was, and how she encouraged and inspired me. I could not keep such valuable lessons to myself. I want this book to convey Asahi's message of hope rather than despair. She might have been physically frail, but she was mentally strong. I wanted to share her strength with you.

To mothers raising children, people with illnesses, people who are struggling for their lives, and to all of us who eventually must face death, I wanted to deliver a message—words of encouragement—from Asahi to each of us. That will make Asahi's nine years live forever in people's minds.

On a personal note, I thought that this book would be the best gift I could give to the girl who loved to read more than anything else. I also thought that by conveying her daughter's wonderful life, this book would bring hope to Asahi's mother, who had lost her dearest daughter. It was Asahi's mother who raised her daughter to rise above her struggles and to shine as brightly as the sun. They both gave me strength I had never known before, and I wanted to show my gratitude to Asahi and her mother.

Asahi loved her mother more than anything in this world. Next to her mother, she talked most about her grandpa, so I wanted them both to be a part of this book. I couldn't be happier that their loving letters appear at the end. I can see Asahi's big smile about that. Above all, if I wrote about her, I thought, Asahi could inspire others just as she had inspired me, and her spirit would continue to live among all kind and warmhearted people who would appreciate and cherish her life forever.

CHAPTER 1

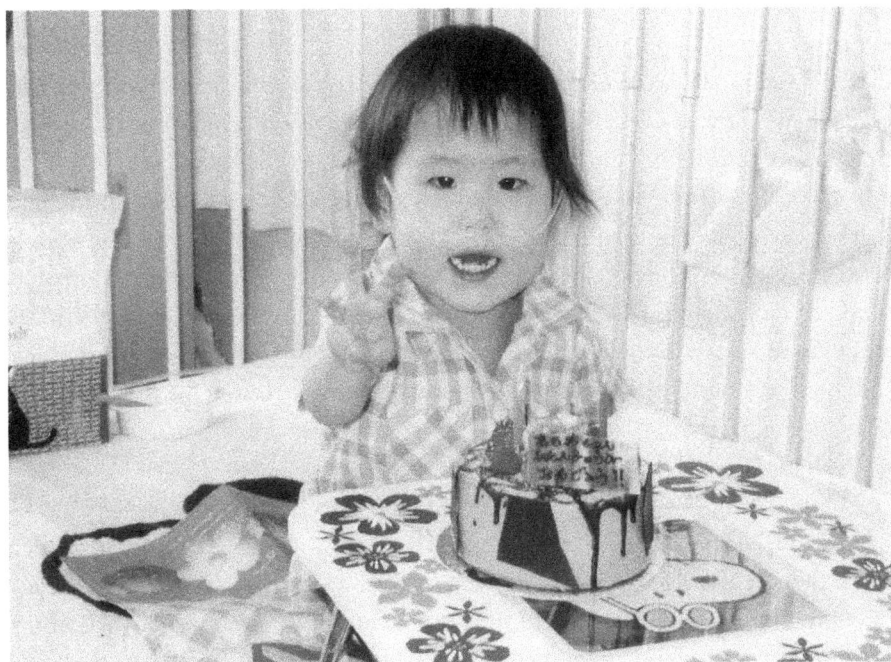

Meeting "the Sun"

Lessons from the Children's Ward

I started doing volunteer work at the hospital in September 2002. I had almost no experience doing such volunteer work and, to be honest, very little confidence that I could be of much help to others.

My motivation to do volunteer work arose from my gratitude towards the doctors and this hospital. You see, in April of that year, I was diagnosed with ventricular tachycardia, a condition caused by the heart arrhythmia I had lived with for ten years. I had nearly lapsed into a coma. Through a referral, I was lucky enough to get an appointment at this hospital, and, in June, a vacancy came up that allowed me to be admitted. Doctors helped to cure the arrhythmia that had plagued me for years. The treatment involved a delicate, non-surgical procedure that, at that time, could not have been performed elsewhere in Japan.

The difference between before and after the operation was miraculous, like a dream. Even six years later, I still could not enter the hospital without a powerful sense of gratitude coming over me—gratitude for the doctors who cured me, for being able to have had such sophisticated treatment at one of the most advanced hospitals in the country, and for being born in Japan, where everyone has equal access to the best medical care at a cost lower than in most other countries. I thought that I would never be able to thank everyone enough, even if I tried all my life.

I learned about the hospital's volunteer program from a pamphlet I had read when I was staying there six years ago. That is how I started to do volunteer work there. I liked to play with children, so I wanted to volunteer as a means of continuing my association with the hospital and showing my appreciation for the doctors. Little did I know that it was I who would be given a great treasure.

Our volunteer work was mainly to play with the children in the playroom, reading picture books, making figures with *origami* (folding papers), and doing other activities. We sometimes studied with those who were supposed to be attending elementary school, and sometimes even counseled children in intermediate school. Their hospital stays varied. Children who stayed for the medical examination often studied, but children who were suffering from serious illnesses generally wanted to play with us.

I had perfect attendance from kindergarten through college, so I never stopped to think how lucky I was to be able to go to school every day. On the contrary, I sometimes wanted to play hooky—just for a day—or I would imagine how happy I might feel if I was absent from school. But since I started volunteer work, I noticed that there were a lot of children who couldn't go to school even though they wanted to. It didn't take long for me to realize how silly and shallow I was.

Many children have to limit their salt and water intake. They not only have to always measure the amount of tea or juice that they drink, but also the soup and miso soup that came with their meals. Realizing such facts, I felt ashamed of my ignorance. They endure so much.

Some children are constantly in and out of the hospital. Some stay for a long time. Some have to give up playing baseball or soccer. One young man, nineteen years old, worried about getting married. He told me that even if he got married, he might not make his wife happy because of his illness. The more time I spent with the children, the more I was moved. They taught me so much. I never expected it, but it did not take me long to realize that I was there to learn, not to do volunteer work.

Fateful Encounter with Asahi

About a year or so after I started doing volunteer work, I came to understand that Asahi was the most seriously ill child in the hospital. She was only three years old when we first met. She was so tiny back then. Looking pale and very tired, she would sit on my knees, breathing through an oxygen tube placed in her nose, and listen to me reading storybooks to her. Little did I know that this tiny girl would come to influence me so profoundly.

One day, Asahi said to me, "My mother told me that I will have an operation that will make my lips pink." She was so happy when she told me the news. Soon after, her purple lips became pink, and she could breathe much more easily than before.

At first, we were not as close as we later came to be. Basically, the patients' privacy was protected, so, as a volunteer, I wasn't told that Asahi would be leaving the hospital to attend school for a few months and then return to the hospital.

On the day she was leaving the hospital, her mother suggested, "Asahi, why don't you take a picture with Mrs. Maeda?"

"Of course!" she said happily.

The photo that we took together is my positive memory of that spring morning. But right after we took the picture, Asahi's face turned gloomy. She looked like she was worried about something, and she anxiously asked me, "I . . . I might return to the hospital. If I do, will you still be here?"

Her mother made signs with her eyes and whispered to me that Asahi was supposed to return to the hospital in autumn. I felt so bad for Asahi and said, "Of course. I will be here for a long, long time!"

We happily celebrated her going home. But when she returned in autumn, she could not leave the hospital again except for an occasional short visit home. Her life was very different from other children's.

The picture we took in the playroom on the day she left the hospital is the only picture we took together. I should have taken more pictures with her. One day in the spring, a happy, six-year-old Asahi was going home and was going to attend school—this moment became the most precious picture in my album.

"Asahi attended school for only one semester when she was a first-grader," her grandfather told me when she became unconscious in January 2008.

I heard that Asahi needed a cylinder of oxygen inhaler on her stroller since she was a baby. She got her first wheelchair when she was three years old, a second one when she was five, and an electric wheelchair when she was seven. I can't forget her smile when we talked about her electric wheelchair.

"Your wheelchair is so beautiful and cute all decorated," I said. "I never saw a colored wheelchair before. The others are all navy blue without patterns."

The moment I told her that, she said, "I have a much better electric one at home!" Her eyes sparkled.

"Really? I would think it's difficult to handle electric ones. Are you able to handle them?"

"Of course! I'm used to it. It didn't take much time at all to learn how to use it. That chair is so convenient and comfortable. I'm very happy with it," she happily replied.

Since it's difficult for small children to handle wheelchairs, the city usually does not permit children to have them, Asahi's mother told me. So, when Asahi got her wheelchair, people who worked at the wheelchair company were surprised. She was the youngest person that the city approved to obtain and operate a wheelchair—and an electric one, at that. At the same time, it made me realize that her illness was much more serious than I had imagined.

Asahi suffered from tricuspid insufficiency, a congenital heart defect that affects one out of one hundred thousand people. The doctor diagnosed her condition when her mother was seven months pregnant with Asahi.

I am told that children who suffer from a tricuspid insufficiency usually have operations at the age of one and can go on to live normal lives. Unfortunately for Asahi, her condition took a sudden turn for the worse two months after her birth, so she needed to have an operation when she was just five months old.

I thought back to when my own children were just a few months old and how my feelings swung back and forth between joy and despair over their ever-changing development. (My baby can hold his head up; my baby can turn over, and so on.) During this same period of development, Asahi battled her severe illness.

Asahi's struggle started even before she was born, which meant her mother's struggle started at the same time. This is why I feel I am less mature compared to Asahi's mother, because mine was a relatively carefree life. Throughout my pregnancy, I was told, "Your baby is fine." My preparing to have a child and Asahi's mother resolving to protect a child separated her and me from the beginning. I thought about the time Asahi's mother was told about her daughter's problem, and I deeply admired her.

I remember her mother calmly saying, "When Asahi was two, her doctor said that it might be her time to go, but she recovered and miraculously lived until she was nine." I was glad that she recovered when she was two. I appreciate from the bottom of my heart her strong will to live and the medical treatment she received from great doctors.

Because she was able to survive that crisis as a child, she was able to grow and develop her wonderful personality and individuality as a person, and she was able to touch my heart so deeply. Without her strong will to live or the best medical treatment, she could not have survived until the age of nine. After Asahi died, her mother told me, "Thanks to the doctors, our family can hold Asahi's funeral ceremony with amazing calm, so I deeply appreciate them."

If Asahi hadn't survived when she was two, she could not have taught me so much. Even though she is no longer with us, because of her miraculous recovery, I have what she has given me. I can't stop thinking, *Asahi! Thank you for making the miracle.*

"Mrs. Maeda, Can You Go to Asahi's Room?"

Mrs. Mori and I were supposed to go to the children's ward to do volunteer work on Friday. Usually, there were seven or eight children in the playroom. They often had oxygen inhalers and IVs on their noses or hands, so it was quite challenging for just two of us to take care of them all.

"Mrs. Maeda, could you play with Asahi in her room?"

"Mrs. Maeda, Asahi is calling you."

I don't know exactly when it started, but nurses began calling me more and more often for Asahi. I felt badly that Mrs. Mori was left to take care of all the other children in the playroom by herself, but I made it a point to go to Asahi's room whenever I was asked to go.

Sometimes, children came to take envious looks into Asahi's room, but nobody complained. Asahi was an exception, so she could request me to her room. That in itself told me that she was extremely ill. She needed an oxygen inhaler and a pacemaker, and had to limit her intake of liquids. She had difficult examinations and treatments—much more than other children—so I wanted to make her life easier and more enjoyable. I decided to do whatever I could for her.

I was born in Osaka, which is famous for its sense of humor. True to form, I have liked to make others laugh ever since I was little. My friends and family think I'm funny, and I especially liked to make jokes when I played with the children in the wards. I was good at making them laugh, and they liked to play with me. I often got carried away when I played with them, however. Even the intermediate- and high-school children were much calmer than I.

I'm a little younger than the other female volunteers, and others tell me that I look young for my age, so children often told me, "We feel like we're playing with a kid, not with an adult lady." I guess this is why Asahi started to ask the nurses to call me more often.

Asahi was also born in Osaka and shared my love for jokes and humor. She often watched comedy programs on TV, and we used to enjoy our time together acting like comedians. She was very witty and her conversation was full of humor.

One day, I imitated a comedian who used a folding fan to make people laugh. The following week, Asahi asked me to copy him again. She had a fan ready for me to use, and even called the doctors and nurses to watch. I had to decline her request, however, explaining to her that my act was a special favor only for her, and that I couldn't do it in front of other people.

I still feel a little embarrassed when I think about mimicking such comedians, but I did it for Asahi because she looked forward to seeing me joke and play every week. When she had to undergo required treatment—such as injections or special diets—I would impersonate her favorite comedians, adapting the lines to fit her situation. I concentrated on making her happy in any way possible. She thought I was very funny playing the role of her spokesman, and she hugged and thanked me. She could not stop laughing. She was also proud and happy when the nurses would tell her, "Asahi, you are very lucky because you can have Mrs. Maeda all to yourself."

When Asahi was feeling better, she was able to play with the other children in the playroom. Much to my regret, however, such opportunities steadily decreased over the years. Children in the hospital have little resistance to germs, so they are allowed into the playroom only when they are well. The same goes for us volunteers. We had to stay away even if we had a slight cold in order not to infect the children.

As for Asahi, who had such a serious condition, nurses had to carefully judge whether to allow her to play with other children. She was often told, "Asahi, you should play in your room today"; "Asahi, you can play in the playroom, but only for half an hour, okay?"

"Then can you send Auntie Maeda to come to my room? I really want to play with Auntie Maeda!" She requested me more and more.

Her long stay in the hospital, limited liquids and salt in her meals, restrictions on where she could play or how long she could play, and sending her friends off when they returned to their homes… When I thought about the things that Asahi went through, I was even more determined to make her happy, even if it was only once a week.

I sometimes made her laugh so much that she almost choked. "I'm really sorry. I'm not a good volunteer," I apologized. When we were playing a game we called "The Shop," I made her laugh too much, so she said, "You are too funny! Since I almost choked, you should stop being the salesperson. It's my turn." Even if we exchanged roles, however, I was still too funny playing the customer, so Asahi sometimes called a nurse who was going through the corridor, and said,

"Auntie Maeda is so funny and I laugh too much, so I have a stomachache." I thought I should be more careful in order not to be fired.

On Friday

Surviving the difficult treatments, Asahi grew stronger each year, but she was still a child. She had likes and dislikes, just like a normal child, such as when it came to food or quarreling with her friends. Once when I was talking to the other children, she got angry and sulked. On another day, when we were playing, she got restless.

"What happened? Are you tired?" As she had a serious illness, I was always worrying about her condition.

"It's nothing. Let's play!"

We started playing again, but she wasn't her usual self. "I got it! You want to go to the bathroom, don't you?" I was right, and she looked sorry because I was right.

"Yes, but if I went to the bathroom now, I'd have less time to play with you, so I'll wait. I won't go."

"You have to go. It's not good for you. I'll come with you and, while you are in the bathroom, I can talk to you from the other side of the door, so you should go!"

"Not in the middle of our play time!" Her stubborn efforts continued.

"If you have time to complain, you should go to the bathroom."

Like this, I often experienced her stubbornness. She never ate snacks that the children got in the morning because she wanted to play with me instead. She said, "Opening a bag of snacks takes time and I don't want to waste my time."

"All right, then, I'll open it for you."

"It's the same thing because while you are opening the snacks, we can't play anyway." She was clever.

Fridays were important to Asahi. Children who stay at the hospital for a long time are taught school subjects by a visiting teacher on an appointed day. I thought that Asahi used to study every Friday, but I hadn't seen her study on Fridays for some time.

"Do you study hard with your teacher these days? I guess you had to skip some lessons, haven't you?" I asked her.

"No! I don't skip them! But I asked my teacher to change my day from Friday to other days. That's a good idea, isn't it? Lucky!" She gave a carefree laugh and made "peace" signs with both hands.

She wanted to play with me as much as she could, so it was a big deal to her how long she could play before I left the hospital. "What time is it now? How many more minutes can you stay?" she often asked. So when I said, "Since you ate well today, I'll give you a bonus: an extra fifteen minutes," she hurrahed. Asahi was so loud that a girl staying in a bed next to hers often scolded her, "Be quiet!"

Asahi had many likes and dislikes in food. This was especially true of her eating pilaf. She did not eat green onions and round onions, even though they were minced. When we took the lid off of the tableware and the meal was pilaf, we looked at each other and sighed, saying, "That's too bad."

Because she had medical instruments such as an IV or oxygen attached to her hands, having a meal was not an easy task for her, so I had to help her pick out the things she didn't like. Picking green onions wasn't so bad, but, "Grains of rice and onions look the same," I told her.

"They are not! Rice is tasty, but onions are bitter!"

"Why don't you eat them? They look the same, and they are good for you."

"What are you talking about? Look, they do not look the same!"

"You can distinguish rice from onions because you have good eyesight, but when you get older like me, rice and onions look the same."

"How strange your eyesight is! All right, then, I will pick onions by myself!"

"That's too bad. You have a hard time enjoying your meal because you have likes and dislikes. If you weren't like that, you could simply enjoy eating, as I do."

"You told me before that when you go to the sushi bar you don't eat fatty tuna and salmon. I remember well! You must not like them! You're denying yourself one of life's great pleasures by not eating fatty tuna and salmon."

Our conversations became heated like that sometimes.

On many occasions, we would talk about her likes and dislikes and it would lead us to playing "Sushi Bar," for both of us liked sushi so much.

Asahi's "Pokemon" Lecture

Asahi's parents used to collect dozens of Pokemon figures for her. She loved the serial comic *Pokemon* and was so happy every time she got a new one.

To tell you the truth, playing with these Pokemon figures with her was the hardest for me.

"Look, I got a new one again!" As soon as I entered her room, Asahi, who was waiting for my visit, stuck her hand with the new figure towards me with great satisfaction.

"Ah, again? Did you get a new one again? I don't know if that's good or bad."

"Of course it's good! I know what you're thinking. It's because you don't want to learn a new name, isn't it?"

"It's difficult for someone my age to learn a lot of new things."

'Don't say that! You've been doing good so far, so don't give up! You have the best memory of all the volunteer ladies."

Why did I need to be flattered by her into learning names? I was inwardly tired of learning, and I almost lost my mind looking at so many figures. One day, I prepared a ''cheat sheet,'' but she quickly noticed what I was doing and scolded me in a commanding tone. ''Mrs. Maeda! It's not right to cheat. Stop cheating!'' Sadly, the sheet was taken from me.

"Yes, yes, Teacher Asahi."

"You should say 'yes' only once, not twice. Let's see...say all the figures' names that you learned last week." She was a perfect little teacher. I made so many mistakes before and we had spent so much time teaching me their names that I was confident that day. I was finally able to recite the names of all thirty figures. I was relieved that I mastered her difficult "Pokemon Lecture," but she continued mercilessly. "Good job! You can advance to the next stage, and you can learn new names. I mean, each has a new name after evolving."

I don't need to learn such troublesome names, I thought, and told her, ''Evolution? I don't want any figures to evolve because I finally learned them all."

"There's nothing we can do about it because they do evolve. Never mind! Don't mind! 'Pichu' is a little mouse, and it becomes 'Pikachu,' and then 'Raichu.' It's interesting, isn't it?"

"It's not interesting at all. It's too difficult." I inwardly felt worried about what would come next. ''What's next?'' I asked, feeling reckless.

"Hikozaru, Moukazaru, Goukazaru...there are many other names, but to-day we must learn these two evolutions or you'll fail my test."

I secretly checked my watch. What good timing—it was time for me to leave. I happily pointed at my watch, but Asahi pretended not to notice and continued with the questions.

"Next! How about 'Pichu'?"

"Pichu…Pikachu…Raichu."

"You can learn, can't you?"

Flattery won't work with me; I inwardly complained and was very tired, but my teacher continued without mercy.

"Mrs. Maeda, how about Hikozaru's evolution? Just try saying them!"

"Hikozaru…Moukaeru ['*kaeru*' means "I'll go home"]…Goukaku ['*goukaku*' means "pass the test"] ni…*shite* [please]."

"No! Hikozaru, Moukazaru, Goukazaru! You are joking, always joking!"

"Teacher! I want to skip this lesson next week." I said this like a child who hated going to school, with the half-crying face.

"What a shame! After learning all the evolved names, you must learn the techniques they use. Skip my lesson? Impossible!" She was shocked. She loved playing school very much, and she was always glad to play with me. But no matter how much she loved it, it was too difficult for me to remember over thirty figures' names, their evolved names, and their techniques. Even if I were younger, it would be impossible.

"When you remember their techniques, then we will finally be able to fight with these figures," she said gladly, but I didn't want to learn and fight in any way. I was fed up with her lectures. As for techniques, Asahi herself needed to look at the instructions very often, so this teacher was unreliable.

However, I thanked her that my memory was trained, my brain got five years younger for sure, and I received nurses' praises. "I can't even remember ten figures' names for my children. Mrs. Maeda, you are great." So I felt good about it.

Now, Asahi is gone and there are no more lectures from her; it's just a fond memory. I even miss that lecture a little and wouldn't mind having her lesson again.

Full of Hope

When Asahi was four or five, she wanted to become a nurse, so she sometimes displayed a nurse's cap that she made with the pieces of white paper beside her pillow. Whenever I put a cap on her and told her, "This cap looks really good on you! You are so kind that you'll be a good nurse," she was so glad.

As she grew older, Asahi regretfully said, "I can't become a nurse because I'm afraid of blood," and changed her dream job to doing other things at a hospital.

"People who work at hospitals have to be kind, patient, and cheerful, so such a job would suit you well," I said.

"Is that right?" She was surprisingly happy to hear me say so. It was not always the same, but she visualized her future full of potential and possibilities.

When Asahi was about eight or nine, she was such a sharp child that I was afraid she might know that her condition was getting worse. But she never asked questions like, "Can I be cured?" or "Do I have a future?" She talked to me about all her problems—even though they were small things—but I never heard a timid or pessimistic word from her.

"Someday, when I'm old and weak, will you take care of me where you work? I will definitely go where you're working." Asahi's eyes sparkled. "When you are old...well, how old are you now?"

When I talk to children, we often go off the subject and it's fun.

"How old do you think I am?" Three other girls who were sharing the room with Asahi looked at me and started guessing: "Thirty-eight!" "I think she is much younger—thirty-two!" "Can't be...about forty-one!" Their voices flew back and forth.

"Wow! I love you all! Thank you."

"You are thanking us, so you must be much older. Oh, Auntie, do you have any children? If you do, please tell me their age." When an intermediate-school student asked me this, Asahi triumphantly said, "I know! Twenty-five and twenty-three!"

"Asahi-chan, why didn't you say so before?" The other girls laughed. On such occasions, I had a rule to give Asahi a quiz.

"Well, then, I have a quiz for you, Asahi!"

"Oh, not again!"

Whenever I said "a quiz," she knew it related to studying, so she disliked this word.

"You said forty-one, but if I were forty-one, how old was I when I had my children?"

"What a nuisance! I hate arithmetic."

Other girls watched from the sidelines cheering Asahi, and Asahi worked on numbers desperately. "It's hard. It's complicated. Your having two children makes it worse!"

"All right. You can do just one at a time."

Finally, Asahi's friend put in a few words to help her out. "Asahi-chan, Mrs. Maeda is not forty-one because that would mean she was only sixteen when she had a baby. That's the same age as I am, a high-school student... It's strange."

"I'm forty-nine now, so try again!" I said.

"It's a pain! I don't even go to school, so I don't need to do arithmetic," Asahi defiantly said to me, but right after that, she remembered and said, "All right. I should be prepared to go back to school. It could happen...you never know, right?"

"Exactly! You have a good memory."

"The great researchers are studying hard until late every day, so miraculous medicines might be discovered, or I might be cured by a great operation, right?"

"Right! It's not a lie. In the old days, we didn't have medicines and operations like we do now. Those were gradually discovered, and we can recover from illnesses that we couldn't before."

When Asahi refused to study before, that was what I had told her. She blinked with a surprised look on her face and said, "Hmmm." Since she was so impressed, I sometimes reminded her of what I had said.

I wanted Asahi to have hope. I didn't want her, who wasn't even ten yet, to think that she had to stay at the hospital forever, so I tried to make her study addition, subtraction, and Chinese characters, even if it was only for a little while.

"I don't want to waste even one second on Fridays when I can play with Auntie Maeda." She even hated to go to the bathroom and refused to eat snacks on Fridays. Therefore, she did not want to study, even if it was for a few minutes; so at first she always got in a bad mood, but this was very important time that I privately named "time for her to have hope for the future."

"As for dreams, I know it's impossible, but...to tell the truth, I wish you were my mother, too. Having my mom and you as a mother also would be the best thing. If it came true, I would be so happy." When she talked about such a dream, leaning on me like a koala, her expression was especially cute.

Her love for her mother was very different from other children's love. For Asahi, her mother was the one who protected her, and they fought against her illness together. It seemed that she thought she was able to fight against her fate if she had her mother. I felt honored that Asahi appointed me as her second mother.

Asahi's mother wrote in the email she sent to me, "Asahi saying that she wants you to become her mother is the highest praise, I think. She probably wants to show her gratitude for your affection by saying that. It means your love is so great that I'm really glad and appreciate you from the bottom of my heart." I was pleased by her words and swore that I would cherish their feeling towards me through my entire life.

Asahi and I talked a lot about her dreams and many other things. She sometimes confided her concerns in me. When she was eight, she started to talk about her concerns about her family. She whispered, "I can't talk about this to anyone but you, so you have to keep this secret. Never tell others, even the nurses, all right?" I always listened to what she had to say and we had serious conversations many times. She knew I talked to her sincerely. She was a person who was able to repay your sincerity; therefore, all the children in the ward loved her.

Names without Titles!

Next to Asahi, a child named Yūki was the one who had to stay in this hospital the longest. When I visited the children's ward for the first time, Yūki took me all over the ward, like a student showing her school to a transfer student.

Although Yūki was four years older than Asahi, they were best friends. As both were staying there for so long, their relationship was like that of sisters. They could say what they wanted to each other and argued with each other like sisters.

"You should get along! You share the same room, so you should be nice to each other."

"Asahi is wrong."

"Yūki doesn't return my toy, so she is wrong."

They often argued with terrible looks on their faces, and it was not easy to arbitrate their arguments. Now that Asahi is gone, however, I can't bear to imagine how lonely Yūki must feel. They not only lived under the same roof, but also shared the loneliness of not having their parents by their side, the anxiety of treatments the night before, and the frustration of being bedridden since they were so young.

When Asahi's mother sent me an email telling me of Asahi's passing, I hurried to the hospital. As soon as Yūki saw me, she asked me in a tearful voice, "Why are you here today? Today isn't Friday. Is it because Asahi is not doing well? Is that right?" Worrying about Asahi, she did nothing but walk around in a corridor that day. Her confusion reflected how deep their relationship was.

A week after Asahi passed away, Yūki ran to me with tearful eyes. It would take a month before she could finally talk about Asahi. But I'm sure Yūki thought about her every day.

"I, I was with Asahi for five years."

I thought, *Me, too,* but could not say anything. Yūki's lonely face wrung my heart. There was nothing I could say to cheer her up, to make her feel better. I knew how deeply they cared for and supported each other. Yūki and I talked about Asahi, and longed for the days we had with her. How was Yūki going to deal with her own illness and the loss of her best friend in her vulnerable teenage years? I wanted to be and should have been there for her.

A few years earlier, they shared the same room for a long time, and both couldn't leave the hospital for even just one night to visit their families while other children got better and left. One day I asked them, "Now I use 'chan' after your name when I call you, but can I call you without 'chan'? Which would you prefer?" They didn't need time to think and simultaneously shouted, with their eyes sparkling, "Without 'chan'!"

In Japan we usually call other's names with respectful titles such as "san" at the end of their names. For children, we use "chan." We call someone's first name without "san" or "chan" only when we have a very close and special relationship, so the children are glad when I call them without "chan."

I remembered, when I was in college, I went to an orphanage for training. There, teachers called children without any honorific titles, like "Hiroshi! Jun!" I remember thinking at the time that addressing each other in that way encouraged a sense of closeness. It was very impressive. It's better for their relationship because children feel that their real parents are calling them. Remembering this from my college training, I asked Asahi and Yūki if I could call them without "chan." Since then, I called them without "chan" out of the many children staying in the hospital.

The other day I received an email from Asahi's mother. "I remember well the day you started calling my daughter without 'chan.' I used to tell her that I liked calling someone only by their first name when we were close, and I have never called Asahi with 'chan,' so Asahi was so glad that she reported to me that Auntie Maeda also called her by her first name only."

The Gift That Arrived Too Late

From time to time, famous people would visit the hospital and meet the children. One day, Asahi told me about one of those visits. "The other day a baseball player, Mr. Iguchi, and other players came here. They were so big and dark. I was kind of scared and not too happy. I love Mr. Kamenashi of 'KAT-TUN' the best."

"Really? Didn't you shake hands with Mr. Iguchi?"

"Of course not. I ran away."

"Oh! That's too bad. If it were me, I would have shaken hands with all the players."

"Then I had an idea," Asahi said. "If I sent a letter to Mr. Kamenashi, he could come see me, so I actually wrote to him, but I forgot to write down this hospital's name, so he won't be coming." She was so upset at herself.

Without telling her, I tried to think of ways I could make her wish come true—a fan club, the TV program 24-Hour TV—Love Saves the Globe, a newspaper company. I had a number of ideas, but didn't do anything about it as time passed.

In the autumn of 2007, I imagined how happy she would be if her dream came true on Christmas, so I sent a letter to B Newspaper Company that had featured an article from me in the past, but there was no response. I wondered if I should try again, or if I should try some other means. I couldn't decide. It was obvious even to me that Asahi's condition worsened in December. I wanted her dream to come true one way or other to cheer her up, but I just could not find a way. Each day I felt more and more frustrated.

If I had any regrets in relation to Asahi, it is this. I don't know whether my regret is that Asahi couldn't see Mr. Kamenashi or if it is because I didn't try hard enough to make it happen. I am not sure, but it is possible that this frustration helped to motivate me to write a book about her life.

Last summer, the newspapers and TV news reported the story about two children from Iraq who stayed in the ward where Asahi was. They recovered, thanks to some delicate operations, and returned to Iraq. It was an impressive story that was reported several times in big articles in B Newspaper Company. I often saw the reporters and wanted to shout out, "There is a child who has been fighting for her life for years in the same ward!"

While the two children from Iraqi stayed in this hospital, I played with them in the playroom. I really cared for them and grew to adore them, and they grew attached to me. They often sat on my knees and sometimes whispered into my ears with their faltering Japanese. I sometimes talked to their fathers, and we shared the joy that their children's operations were successful. I was really happy to see them well and to see their smiles. Iraqi children who had no access to good medical care came to Japan, got better, and returned to Iraq saying, "I want to visit Japan again."

I was moved to see the high medical standards at this hospital and the skills of its hardworking doctors that had brought such welcomed results. I saw that with my own eyes. It was wonderful news that all of us in Japan could be proud of.

If other newspapers featured this story, they would have handled it similarly, I think. Still, I could not help but feel some frustration as I read the repeated articles about the success of the operations. Every time I read them, I had a kind of empty feeling, probably because I thought about Asahi, who had been fighting for years without being reported on by anyone. I also thought about the doctors who devoted themselves to their patients, but never received any kind of acknowledgement.

It's been reported that there are fewer and fewer acute care physicians in Japan every year. I understand that sensational news attracts attention, but I couldn't help but wonder why the media didn't write articles about the doctors who take care of children with heart diseases, too. If the media wrote about the doctors in this hospital, which is the best heart disease center in Japan—and if reporters had paid some notice to Asahi—perhaps I might not have felt as frustrated as I did.

I had hoped that Asahi would meet Mr. Kamenashi and could imagine her excitement if it came to be, but I gave up trying after sending only one letter. I wish I had done more—regardless of how I would have looked—and became

"Santa Claus" for Asahi so she could have had a wonderful last Christmas. Because I couldn't give her a great gift, the phrase, "Asahi, I'm sorry," will always echo in my mind.

Special Charms

All of the hospital volunteers wore the same aprons and nametags, but my nametag had a tiny handmade paper "sandwich" and a light blue charm inside.

One Christmas Day, at lunchtime, I told Asahi, "You look so contented with your delicious lunch that I am hungry now." Asahi quickly made me a "sandwich" by pasting small pieces of green, pink, and red paper between white triangular papers about three or four centimeters. "These are cucumber, ham, and tomato," she explained happily. "You are taking care of us while we are eating, so please help yourself if you are hungry."

It was so well made, even if Asahi was only four at the time. I pretended to eat it gladly, and she was very satisfied with me. Other children who were watching us gathered and said to me, "Well, I will make something for you! I will give you this sticker!"

Now, I have so many stickers on my nametag you can barely see my name and picture. Some children put a sticker on my tag on the day they leave, saying, "It means that we are friends, so please keep it on your tag forever." They looked so cute as they tried to put stickers on my nametag, standing on their tiptoes, that I'd want to see them again but, on the other hand, since it's a hospital, I wished that they never returned.

Asahi made the light blue charm, too. Light blue was her favorite color. It was just a few centimeters, made of *origami* paper with a pretty pattern, and she wrote the word "charm" on it. Whenever other children find the charm in my nametag, they are amazed at how well made it is and speak highly of it. "Wow! It looks so real!"

A lot of people gave Asahi charms, praying for her to get well, so she knew very well the power of prayer from those who loved her. "Here, this is for you, Auntie Maeda."

"Thank you. It looks like a real one. Good job! This charm is going to work because you made it for me."

Asahi didn't add any explanation about it then, but later her grandfather told me, "She loved to create things; she was always making something. She said that charms were special, however, and she only gave her charms to very special people."

When I found out about the meaning of her charm, she was already unconscious. "Asahi, you gave me a charm because you thought of me as a special person."

The charm is small but very valuable to me because Asahi put her heart into making it. Every time I look at it, I remember her hardship, her strength with kindness, and her ability to live cheerfully in the hospital ward, and those thoughts encourage me.

Asahi's Busy Schedule

How bored she must be! I thought, because Asahi had to stay in the hospital for years. She used to say, however, "My grandpa always laughs and says, 'Why are you so busy when you shouldn't be?' But I am really busy."

Why was Asahi so busy? Of course, she had to have her temperature checked, her weight recorded, and other examinations and treatments every day. Besides those, however, Asahi's schedule was filled with her effort to express her gratitude to her parents, grandparents, doctors, nurses, and even to me. She was the type of child who wanted to express her appreciation.

When her mother's birthday drew near, Asahi started thinking about what sort of gift she could give her. One day, as soon as I arrived at her room, she told me in her cheerful Osaka dialect what she decided to give her mother.

"I've decided! I'll make a handmade picture book for her."

"Wow, that's amazing! Can you make that?"

"Sure can, and I will! And one more thing. I'll give her another gift."

"Oh, that's so extravagant! What is it?"

"It's a secret."

She was so excited that I do not have words to describe how excited she was. I was moved that she would celebrate her mother's birthday with such heartwarming kindness. *Asahi's consideration is the best gift. It's more than enough!* I thought. I felt a little envious of Asahi's mother.

She was pleased with her idea. She had been thinking about the gifts for a long time, and she finally found them. She immediately started to make her original picture book so she could finish it before her mother's birthday. She didn't tell me what it was that went with the picture book, saying only, "You will find out!" I had to wait for her to tell me later.

A few days passed, and she finished her picture book. It was an innocent book handmade by Asahi. Although it only had a few pages, it looked like a real book with pages that you could turn. The book contained some cute drawings and a short story about a day that Asahi and her mother spent together. I thought how happy she must have felt to spend such a wonderful day with her mother—her favorite person in the whole world—away from the hospital. As I turned the pages, tears welled up in my eyes just thinking about it.

"I can tell you what the other gift is now." Asahi opened a drawer next to her bed and gently and proudly showed me another gift. It was clumsily wrapped with beautiful wrapping paper. *Where did she get the paper?* I wondered.

"I already wrapped it, so you can't open it. The gift is something you know, though."

"What is it? It's fairly big and soft. I can't guess."

"Do you give up?"

"Yes, I don't want to give up, but I give up."

"This—this is the cushion," she told me.

"Your mother will cry!"

"Oh, but I don't want her to cry. I want to make her happy," she said. But Asahi was so smart that she could understand that "cry" meant "cry for joy." She looked very satisfied that she could make her mother so happy. The cushion was Asahi's favorite. She used to hold it in her arms while she watched TV. "When my mother visits me at the end of the day after work, she lies down with the cushion, and sometimes she actually falls asleep."

"Really? That cushion is your treasure—something that you are proud of. You always said that it is so soft, there is no other cushion like it anywhere."

"It's all right, it's all right! If my mom has this cushion, she can sleep comfortably. I'm going to give this one no matter what! I've already decided!" Her resolve was so firm. I gave her a gentle pat on her head and praised her. "You are really sweet." I almost cried, even though I was not her mother.

She opened the drawer often to check that her gift was safe until the birthday. "I wonder whether my gift is crushed or out of shape? Oh, no, it's fine. I feel better." She smiled contentedly. I was excited, too, because I could imagine how happy Asahi's mother would be with those gifts, and I wanted to know all the details.

On the first Friday after the birthday, as soon as I saw Asahi, I asked, "How was your mother's birthday?"

"You were right. Mom was so happy she even cried a little. Successful, successful!"

The thing is, this was nothing out of the ordinary for Asahi, who continued to impress me time and again with her thoughtfulness, like Valentine's gifts for Grandpa and Dad, letters for friends leaving the hospital, and surprises for the nurses. So I understood why she, who must have been bored, always said, "I'm busy, I'm busy!" Her heart was always filled with thanks and gratitude.

Just before she went home for a short visit—her last visit home—she must have been very tired, but she made a bead necklace for me without a moment's rest for two days. I get a lump in my throat whenever I think about her making the necklace, because it had so many beads. She had to put her heart and soul in making it, carefully threading each bead.

Asahi put a lot of thought into how she expressed her gratitude to people who had taken care of her. It was exciting for her, so I was always glad to hear about it. She often wondered, "Which is better, a letter or a gift? If it's a gift, which is better? My favorite sticker or a handmade gift?"

Although I saw her only once a week, she appreciated me so much. When I think about how considerate she was and how much time she spent making gifts to show me her gratitude, I am moved to tears. Now I keep these special mementos—a scarf and an accessory case knitted by hand, a handmade sticker that says, "I love Auntie Maeda," letters in which she wrote, "Will you play with me again?"—in a pretty box especially for them.

"I want to go to Disneyland again!"

"I want to go on a picnic again!"

"I want to go to Pokemon's event."

Asahi probably had a lot of places she wanted to go and a lot of things she wanted to do, but she never longed for anything she couldn't attain, and she concentrated solely on what she could do to enjoy that moment. It was her way of living. Out of all the people, she could be the most bored, but she seemed to be happy doing things she could do on the bed.

"I'm busy. After I finish this, I have to make a gift for my mom, then Grandpa and Grandma. Oh, I'm so busy!"

I remember a line by a Japanese famous poet, Mr. Mitsuo Aida, "The faster a top spins, the quieter it is."

CHAPTER 2

The Family Who Raised "the Sun"

Grandpa's Love

I spent a lot of time reading books with Asahi.

When I was an apprentice teaching kindergarten in my college days, I was praised by an older teacher who was highly respected in the field of child education. "The way you read to children is very good. Their eyes sparkle when you read." She praised me in front of the children, and I still remember her calm voice very well.

About twenty years had passed since I read books to my children, so I was glad I could read books to children again in the hospital.

Asahi gradually got attached to me and would lean on me as she listened to me read. She always held my arms with both hands, so she looked like a little koala bear. We chose books to read according to her condition and feelings. If she liked a story, she sometimes asked me to read the same book several times a day.

Two of her favorite books were *Chakkuri Kakisu* and *Onchorori, Nezumikyo* by Mr. Masao Kogure. She loved for me to read these humorous books. "The way you read is so funny! One more time, please!" I probably read these books over one hundred times. She had a better memory than me and recited those stories word for word. If I made a mistake while reading, she corrected me right away.

I wanted to make Asahi laugh, so I read books in an exaggerated style. I changed my voice and tone to fit the story. Even when she was not feeling well and could hardly open her eyes, she would lie on the bed and enjoy my reading.

A year or two after Asahi and I became close, I noticed that there were a lot of books from the library in a paper bag by her bed. These were changed regularly. The bag was always full, so I imagined how heavy it must be to carry. Later, I found out that the books were delivered by her grandpa, whom Asahi always talked about.

I learned that Asahi read about three thousand books in nine years. Her grandpa probably calculated it from the number of books he could borrow per week. I was very surprised with both of them—one who patiently delivered so many books he borrowed from the library and one who read them all.

"I knew about Asahi's illness before she was born," her grandpa explained, "so I wondered what I could give or teach Asahi. *How about English?* I thought. But after further thought, I decided that reading books was the most helpful way to expand her world. I wanted her to experience what she couldn't experience herself by reading." I was moved by his love and how desperately he longed for his granddaughter's happiness.

"I tried hard to select appropriate books for Asahi. I avoided books related to death, choosing exciting, enjoyable, and tender books instead. When Asahi got older, she had already read almost all the books at the library, so it was difficult to find new books for her. It took about one hour for me to choose books."

After it got too hard to find books from one library, Asahi's grandfather found another and began borrowing books from two libraries. When he told me this story, my heart was filled with warmth at the thought of Asahi's wonderful grandpa seeking so many treasures for her.

Her grandpa told me all this in Asahi's room after she had fallen into a coma. It was hard for everyone. He continued talking about their lives. "I think that 'obstacle' is one characteristic, not unhappiness. I raised her with that belief in me. Now she is unconscious, but if she wants to live longer, she will live. If she feels she's had enough, she will leave. I consider our human life span in such a way."

His eyes filled with tears, but his voice remained strong, and—although I was not a family member but just a volunteer—he inspired me with his words.

Although Asahi spent most of her life confined to the children's ward, she learned a lot. She was so smart that she not only had knowledge but also kindness, patience, and cheerfulness. She was all of these things—much more so than healthy children who can attend school every day. I admired the fact that she could learn what's important in life.

Besides delivering over three thousand books to Asahi so she could expand her world through reading, her grandpa delivered them brimming with affection. If not for her grandpa, Asahi would probably not have been the person she was.

Grandma's Love

Asahi was surrounded by people who loved her. "I really appreciate everyone giving Asahi their affection. It fueled her spirit, so she could live and shine," her mother said modestly—and she was right.

No matter how much affection a person receives, however, it would make no difference if he or she couldn't understand or appreciate it and was not happy.

Asahi always appreciated the love she received from others, and felt happy. Although she was just a child, she could really feel the affection and sincerity of others ten or a hundred times more than the rest of us.

Whenever Asahi spoke about the doctors and nurses who took care of her, her parents, her grandparents, teachers, friends, and volunteer women, her eyes were pure.

Next to her mother, I definitely believe that Asahi's maternal grandmother loved Asahi the most. Even before Asahi was born, she knew that her daughter's unborn baby had a serious heart problem. Then, for nine years after Asahi was born, Grandma supported her daughter through her hardships. It is much more than I can describe in this book, but knowing about her, I had to mention it.

Asahi's grandma's life changed completely after Asahi was born. Asahi's parents were still young and had to move to be near her grandparents. Grandma worried about her daughter and granddaughter. Although she was filled with anxiety, she could not just sit around and worry; she had to cheer them up. If it were not for her grandmother's love, Asahi could not have lived as happily as she did. Asahi repaid Grandma's efforts in her own way by showing her deep gratitude to others, which was the best repayment Asahi could give.

"My ba-ba [grandma] runs a small Japanese restaurant. The Japanese white radish in her oden stew is the most delicious in the world! The taste of her radish is so different from what they feed us here," Asahi would say when she ate Japanese white radish at the hospital. Her grandmother was very busy running the restaurant and—when Asahi did go to school—taking her to or picking her up from nursery school or elementary school.

Asahi's grandma often played with her. I was very surprised to hear that although Asahi was sick, her grandma didn't hesitate to discipline her. Even though she was busy, Grandma welcomed Asahi's friends with snacks and went to buy cakes for them whenever they came over. She gave a lot of love when Asahi was home.

Grandma must have really wanted to visit Asahi in the hospital, but she was busy running her restaurant and keeping up the family business so that her husband and her daughter could go see Asahi as much as they could. She was like a catcher in baseball—the quietest, but most important, position. She took care of her family so that they all could do what they had to do without any worries.

And I believe Asahi knew how much Ba-ba loved her and could tell me all about her grandmother's love.

I have a daughter, so I can imagine Asahi's grandmother's love, but there is no way I can express in words the depth of her grandma's grief and the tears she shed at Asahi's funeral ceremony. I've never seen such emotional tears in my life. Asahi's grandmother's and mother's love for her was so deep.

Asahi understood her grandmother's love. Although she gave her grandmother a great deal of anxiety, she also made her very happy.

The Mother Who Raised Asahi to Be 'the Sun'

I only met Asahi's mother a few times. But because Asahi talked a lot about her in a frank and honest manner, I could tell how her mother raised her. I found later that Asahi's mother was as wonderful a person as I expected her to be and that was due to the influence of Ji-Ji (Asahi's grandpa) on her.

One day, Asahi and I were playing house, and I noticed how good she was at using her knife.

"How did you learn how to use a knife?" I asked her.

"My mom taught me. I always cut vegetables when we cook curry rice at home," she answered cheerfully.

"Isn't it dangerous for you to use a knife?" I remembered that she was taking medication to aid the circulation of her blood, so I was afraid if she cut her fingers, it would be difficult for the bleeding to stop.

"It's all right! Mom told me to curl my fingers when I use a knife, and that as long as I do that I won't cut my fingers," said Asahi.

"You have a great mother," I told her. Asahi's mother taught her how to deal with problems and made her challenge everything without fear of failure.

When Asahi went to Tokyo Disneyland with her parents, she had so much fun and had so much to tell. The car ride was so long that she got very tired on the way back, but she had enjoyed herself so much that she came back extremely happy. If, like me, her parents had been afraid that such a strenuous adventure would be bad for Asahi, I wouldn't have seen her eyes sparkling that day. "I even took an amusement ride, the scary kind! I thought my heart was going to stop." The girl with a critical heart ailment gave a carefree laugh.

I thought it was very brave of them to take a child who needed an oxygen tank and a wheelchair to crowded places. *If I were Asahi's mother*, I thought, *she easily might have been a more timid and withdrawn child.* Asahi's mother, on the other hand, took her everywhere and raised her as a brave and healthy child.

"We all wanted to take pictures with Mickey, Minnie, and other characters, so we went to them, but Disneyland was so crowded that we had to wait our turn for a long time. But, because I was in a wheelchair and probably stood out or something, the characters found me even from far away and came to me. I took a picture with my favorite characters, Chip and Dale, too, so I was very lucky," she told me happily.

I had spent enough time with Asahi to know that she was innocent and honest, so I knew that she wasn't kidding or making things up. The picture she took at Disneyland was on the New Year's card she sent me. Her beautiful smile was so memorable that I'll keep that card as my treasure.

Asahi never thought less of herself because she was restricted to a wheelchair and tied to an oxygen tank. She never envied others. On the contrary, when people describe her, children and adults both say she was "tender and kind." I credit that to Asahi's mother being a "tender and kind" person. She raised Asahi to "enjoy where you are and what you have; don't compare yourself with others." These may sound like simple lessons, but they are difficult to teach.

There is a picture of Asahi and her mother wearing *yukata* kimonos at a Summer Festival. Asahi has one of her big smiles on her face. I was afraid that the crowd and smoke from the fireworks would be bad for her, but the smiles on Asahi's and her mother's faces dispelled my anxiety. The picture only proved that they had a wonderful time.

Considering Asahi's stamina, Kyushu was too far, I thought, but then I heard she went to an amusement park there. Her mother even took her to the huge Kyocera Dome to enjoy an event featuring her favorite Pokemon. She talked about that experience many times, and each time she couldn't wait to tell me how much fun she had.

Asahi's mother worked full time and must have been busy and tired, but she took the time to have Asahi experience different events, like any other healthy child. She made every effort to make Asahi happy, and Asahi—always extroverted and confident—didn't worry about what other people might think because she needed a wheelchair and the oxygen inhaler.

"The oxygen tank helps me. It's my friend. With it, I feel comfortable," she often said.

"Do you want to take it away when you take pictures?" her mother asked, but Asahi didn't care. All of the pictures she gave me were of her smiling and posing with "peace" hands and the oxygen tank on.

Her Long-Awaited Visit Home

Children who are confined to a hospital are very happy when they are allowed to go home—even if it's for a few days. At home, they can completely depend on their parents and probably have a lot of toys of their own.

From what I could tell, Asahi especially looked forward to three highlights whenever she went home. One was that she was able to go to her favorite sushi bar; another is that she could play with her dog, Niko (Niko was named by Asahi after "*nikoniko*," which means "smiling" in Japanese). She was most excited about the third thing, which was that her mother would bring new clothes for her to wear whenever she went home. Asahi's mother always splurged on new clothes for her. It must have been a reward from the mother for her daughter, who stayed in the hospital almost all year wearing pajamas. Asahi's mother brought them several days before Asahi went home. Whenever she had permission to go home, Asahi showed me all her clothes, which she neatly folded by herself. "These are the clothes I'm going to wear this time!" she told me.

"Wow! How pretty these are! Your mother has such good taste. It's nice of her to buy you new clothes every time. You're so lucky! You are going home with these boots? Don't catch a cold so you can go home." I spoke with exaggerated gestures as usual and would lay out all her clothes on the bed in order, from head to toe. "Look! It looks like Asahi's sleeping with her clothes on."

"Really! I even have a hat on!" She loved to see how I laid down her clothes.

Then I would put her cute little jeans on my arms and put her pair of socks on my hands, saying, "Let me wear them!"

"That's not how you wear them!" she would point out. Because I did this on purpose every time her mother brought her clothes, she was expecting me to do this and always laughed hard looking at her jeans on my arms.

"Mom bought me sandals! A jacket with a parka, too." Asahi's mother probably splurged on new clothes for her daughter because Asahi rarely had the chance to wear daily outfits. Fashion is the most fun for girls, so Asahi's mother let Asahi enjoy the latest fashion, even if she had to stay in the hospital almost all year. She never thought, *Oh, just put on a coat over your pajamas. We are driving.* I admired that she did everything she could for her daughter.

Asahi's mother emailed me recently and told me about the clothes Asahi wore when she went home. "She was looking forward to seeing your reaction when you saw her clothes, so she begged me to bring them by Thursday because you came on Friday."

She continued, "There are so many other things I want to tell you, like how happy Asahi was when you praised her, how she wanted to please you and how hard she worked at it, and how she asked if she could talk to you about something."

Her saying so touched my heart. "I want to please, I want to be recognized, I want to be praised." These desires are very important in a child's growth. Knowing that I had occupied such a place in Asahi's heart, I was moved to tears thinking of Asahi, who had gone to heaven.

Even when Asahi had permission to go home for a visit, her health didn't always allow it. So, when she had permission, I prayed that she would stay well.

On rare occasions, she was actually able to leave the hospital (not a visit to her home), and she came to the hospital as an outpatient. When she had an appointment on Friday, she would come up to the fifth floor of the children's ward. "I came here to see Auntie Maeda!"

One day, Asahi was so proud that she and her mother were wearing matching checked shirts. "Look, look! I am wearing matching shirts with Mom!" No doubt Asahi was happy, but Asahi's mother was probably much happier. I guessed that she must have wished that she could have such happiness forever.

Mothers who have sick children are truly strong. I remember the story my daughter told me when she was in the first grade. They were on their way to school when some boys asked a mother who was pushing her daughter's wheelchair, "Which time in your life did you like the best?"

"I love now the best because I can go to school every day with you guys," the mother answered.

"Tacchan's mother seemed to be very happy," my daughter said. Even though she was a young child, she probably admired this mother's positive thinking, and so did I.

I think mothers who have sick children learn things from the children they are caring for. They have strength we mothers with healthy children don't have. Every time I speak with young mothers in their twenties or thirties at this hospital, they give me a lot of courage—and Asahi's mother stood out among them.

One day, Asahi complained, "Listen! I have a pacemaker. I told my Mom before, 'I hate having a pacemaker in here.' She told me, 'What are you talking about? If it were not for the pacemaker, you would die.'"

"It means that you won't die as long as you have a pacemaker. Aren't you lucky!" I told her.

She seemed to be relieved with my words and laughed innocently, saying, "You're right!" But to tell you the truth, I was shocked to hear what Asahi's mother said.

Asahi's mother changed her daughter's thinking from "I hate my pacemaker" to "thanks to a pacemaker, I can live." She had amazingly positive thinking. I think it takes courage to tell a small child, "If you didn't have it, you would die." But she never compromised, even though her daughter was ill, and she always explained the facts without any hesitation so that Asahi could understand.

On another occasion, I asked Asahi, "When is your birthday?" I was surprised at what she said.

"September 11. Is that a scary day when terrorism occurred?"

She was only seven at the time, and she looked worried.

"Did your mother tell you that?" I asked. I was right. "She talks to you about such difficult matters, doesn't she?" *What a wonderful mother she is*, I thought. It's easy to tell a small child, "Your birthday is the same as Christmas Day," or, "Your birthday is on Hinamatsuri [Girls' Day]," but it's very difficult to say, "Your birthday is the day terrorism occurred." In such ways, Asahi's mother surprised me many times, and I admired her for that.

"Your mother tells you everything, even it's a hard thing to tell, so I think your mother is great."

"Don't you know about that terrorism?"

"Yes, a terrible incident happened in America that day. After that, however, people of the world have come to reflect about their lives—especially on the anniversary of September 11. We think of things like we should be kind to others and treasure our lives, or we should try to do our best every day, so September 11 is a very important day for us," I replied, avoiding saying anything about so many lives being lost in a split second. I thought that would be too cruel to say to a child who treasured her life more than anyone.

"I see. So the day is scary, but it's all right that I was born on the same day, right?"

"That's right. You were born on a very important day, and it's good that your mom talked to you about things like that."

Asahi was relieved to hear that. September 11 is the day people of the world think about the importance of life. Her birthday fell on a day that was just right for her, who treasured life.

Fun on a Special Diet

Children who must limit their liquid intake need to be aware of the amount of liquid they have in a day. So, they record every time they have a cup of tea, juice, or water, and figure out how much more liquid they can have. Asahi said, "I want to drink now, but if I do, I'll suffer later." Asahi was always thinking about the amount of her liquid intake. Sometimes, a special meal for kidney patients was added to her already strict diet.

I guessed that special meal was lightly seasoned. It was quite obvious that the rice was different from the white rice that we eat. It looked like glue and looked so unappetizing in a rice bowl. She was already used to this rice, so she could afford to laugh and say, "This is actually awful."

But I always thought to myself, *Poor thing!* "I'm an expert in making *onigiri* [rice balls]," I said, "so I'll make appetizing rice balls! So you try to eat!" I expected her to react, and she didn't disappoint me.

"E—e—expert?" Instantly she answered back like a comedian. That's because we talked many times before about my being all thumbs.

Mrs. Mori and I always said, "Don't request difficult *onigiri*-making from these volunteer women on Friday." That's because three women on Wednesday were good at using their hands, and, of course, Asahi knew the difference between us. She used to request, "Please make me a character-shaped *onigiri*." But those days, her expectations of me were much lower, so she expected only the shape of "circle, triangle, square, heart, rabbit, dog, and bear."

"Is this a dog or a bear?" she asked.

"It's up to you."

"What kind of answer is that?"

The very woman who made it couldn't say what it was. They all looked the same, so if I meant it to be a rabbit, I added some carrots on it, and she was really pleased to eat that.

"I tell you what, Auntie Maeda. Even if your *onigiri* is just a round one, I still like your *onigiri* the best. You tell me a lot of interesting stories while I eat, so I like eating with you the best." She complimented me with an innocent face. How many of my clumsily made *onigiri* did she eat?

If I were Asahi, I wouldn't be happy with the special kidney meal, but, to my surprise, she didn't hate it. She always tried to find the positive rather than negative side of things.

"This meal tastes awful, but I'm fortunate to be able to eat." It's surprising that a young child would say so. I guessed that this thought came from her wonderful grandpa's education. What she said next was very cute. "With this meal, I can have a cup of ice cream. You envy me, don't you?" She waved her ice cream cup slowly in front of my face on purpose.

Since we had known each other for a long time then, she knew very well that I liked the "rich milk flavor" of Haagen-Dazs best of all. So, pretending to be serious, I told her, "You have no idea!"

"I'm really lucky! With the regular meals, there is no ice cream, but with this special kidney meal, there is a Haagen-Dazs!"

Even though to keep her calories balanced she couldn't have a full cup of ice cream, she loudly and slowly emphasized the word "Haagen-Dazs" and enjoyed seeing my envious face. What a delightful child!

"Here is a question for you! Which would you prefer—no snack with regular-tasting rice or Haagen-Dazs with awful rice?"

"Haagen-Dazs with regular-tasting rice!" I shot back.

"I didn't give you such a choice! You're always kidding!"

With this special meal, Asahi sometimes had a chocolate-flavored snack in addition to the Haagen-Dazs. I coveted the Haagen-Dazs, but she preferred the chocolate snack to ice cream.

She shouted, "*Banzai!*" raising both her hands. "Hooray! Today there is a chocolate snack, too! My mom loves this snack very much. Because I can have some desserts, I can endure special meals."

"You say your mom loves it, but aren't you going to eat it?"

"No! Mom likes it very much, so I always save it to give to her."

"And does your mom eat your precious snack?"

"Sure! She looks so happy."

Asahi looked so happy saying so. I knew that Asahi loved to see her mother's happy face more than anything, but I was surprised that a small child would give her mother her own snack.

Asahi's mother was great, too. I could see her enjoying the snack Asahi gave her without hesitation, probably giving Asahi a compliment: "It's so yummy! You are so kind. Thanks to you, I feel strong now!" She didn't put anything before her daughter's feelings, wanting only for Asahi to experience the joy of making her mother happy. It taught me that we shouldn't hesitate to teach children how to make others happy.

Asahi's mother always thought, *What's the most important thing for my daughter? What does she want to do now?* Even though her daughter was a sickly child, she always treated Asahi as an equal.

At the end of a hard day's work, she visited Asahi and treasured every moment of it. Although Asahi's mother is much younger than me, she impressed me so much with her superhuman effort. I raised healthy children and depended on my husband for a great deal of material and mental support.

"If you didn't have a pacemaker, you might die."

"Asahi's snack is so yummy."

Asahi's mother always talked to her daughter frankly and without hesitation. She taught Asahi so many important things about life. Therefore, Asahi was who she was—a kind, strong, cheerful child who was never jealous and who always wished others happiness.

One day, Asahi said, "My mom often scolds me for crying. She asks, 'What are you crying for?' If crying helps, yes, I can cry, but not if I cry too often for something that crying doesn't help."

I am quick to cry, so what Asahi's mother said struck a chord with me. "Does your mother say so? She is great. I am easily moved to tears. Doesn't she cry?"

"She said it's okay to cry when someone passes away, or when I watch TV and I am moved. But we shouldn't cry when we have to think or explain the situation." Strict, yet warm and wonderful. That's who Asahi's mother is. I suppose that ever since Asahi was born, her mother had been spurring her on in such a way to make her stronger.

"What good does it do to cry?" What this young mother said was very dignified and will keep encouraging me from that day on.

A Three-Legged Race with Mom

It's not surprising for young children to love their mothers, but Asahi's love for her mother was stronger than most. Her mother often said, "Asahi loves me so, so much." Asahi probably understood that her mother was the one who would fight with her against her illnesses.

An email Asahi's mother sent me later clearly explained how the two of them fought to overcome Asahi's illness together:

As Asahi grew older, she grew to fear the painful treatments when she found out about them. Before she was five, we didn't tell her about the treatments in advance because she hated them so much. She wanted me to tell her about the treatments, however, so, with the hospital's cooperation, I tried not to let Asahi know about it until the day of the treatment. But she began to sense it on her own or sometimes hospital staff would mention it accidentally. When that happened, she became very upset, so I needed to talk to her about it. After going back and forth for a while, I accepted her terms. Asahi won. We decided that I would let her know about the treatment the day before and stay with her overnight.

Parents are not allowed to stay with children in the hospital, but Asahi had so many catheter treatments that they made it an exception for us. Still, she sometimes heard about it from someone else and it would upset her again. So we talked, again and again. Finally, we decided that I would let her know three days before the treatment. I tried to explain and persuade her step-by-step about everything in this way. It wasn't always easy to explain things to her because, as she matured, she didn't always accept what I told her. I therefore had to change the way I explained things according to her age. It was hard to explain things to her, but I could understand her growth very well.

The day you saw Asahi crying in the hallway was the hardest. That day, we told her about the treatment on the day of the treatment. But, more than that, she was crying because it was Friday, the day you came. "It's Friday, and I can't play with Auntie Maeda." She was crying fiercely; it was very hard. As I knew Asahi would be disappointed, I wanted her treatment to be any day but Friday, but once a treatment is scheduled, it's hard to change, and she needed to have it done. Later, when I started to tell her about the treatments in advance, she was so disappointed if they were on Friday. She would say, "Then it must be in the afternoon." But as for morning, it took three times longer to persuade her.

Asahi and I struggled to come to an agreement as to how and when to tell her about the treatments, but once promises were made and promised kept, she did not complain. I, as a parent, am so proud of her for her effort and strength.

Reading this email, I could understand how her mother watched Asahi grow up and how she patiently dealt with Asahi as she matured. With a combination of both tenderness and strictness, she always grasped Asahi's feelings and her level of understanding as they fought together against her illness. I knew she had a very hard time, but this email told me more than just about her hardship. She said, "I could understand Asahi's growth very well." She praised Asahi. "She was amazingly strong, and I am very proud of her as a parent for her effort and strength." I guess that Asahi knew her mother was fighting with her. She probably understood that every time she overcame her hardship, it made her mother happy and proud.

Asahi's mother wrote, "The day you saw Asahi crying in the hallway was the hardest." When I arrived at the children's ward that Friday, Asahi's bed was being moved from an examination room to her room. I could hear her crying even from a distance.

"Asahi, Auntie Maeda is here."

Asahi stopped crying when her mother and nurses told her I had come, and everyone laughed at her sudden change in demeanor. Later, I learned that the reason Asahi cried so hard even after the treatment was not because she felt pain or was scared, but because she wasn't told about the treatment. "Aren't you lucky that your treatment finished before Auntie Maeda left?" Asahi's mother said, and Asahi finally calmed down.

Returning to her room after the treatment, Asahi looked dazed and had no energy to play, probably due to a combination of being afraid of the treatment, being upset from not being told about it until the last minute, crying so hard, and, perhaps, due to medication. All I could do was stay by her bed and tell her, "You did well. I will stay with you a little longer." That day, Asahi's mother also looked so exhausted. I felt responsible for causing so much trouble for everyone because I came on Friday. After that day, no treatment was done without telling Asahi in advance.

Asahi's mother's role was not only being a "mom" but also a "comrade." She endured all the hardships Asahi endured. Asahi's love for her mother was not as simple as other children's love for their mothers. It was full of gratitude and respect. I can't possibly become such a strong mother, and it's a shame that I don't have the confidence or strength in myself to overcome difficulties like Asahi. But from now on, when I encounter troubles, I will hear in Asahi's unique Osaka dialect, "Auntie Maeda! Don't be discouraged," and she will inspire me. Now, I take her life to heart and try to follow her example.

When I say, "Asahi was very strong," people sometimes ask, "Didn't she cry?" She had to go through a lot of treatments that even adults can't bear, so of course she cried, and she cried loudly. It was very difficult for nurses and me to comfort her. Sometimes I didn't know what to say. I knew she was the exact opposite of a spoiled child who didn't listen to others. So what words could I say to such a child who had endured so much more than other children?

I couldn't simply say, "Hang in there!" I held her hands and praised her for being brave. "You have had so many painful treatments; you don't want to do this anymore, do you?" At that moment, Asahi stopped crying and seemed to think about her mother. Then I said, "Your mom must be proud of you. She would say, 'Good job, Asahi! I knew you could do it.'"

Asahi's expression softened and it showed a note of resolution. She probably thought, *If it makes Mom proud of me, then I can do it again!* Asahi's mother had struggled so desperately with her daughter and Asahi knew that, so even though her mother wasn't there, she was able to give Asahi the strength she needed. What matters is not if the person can stay beside you when you need her; what matters is if we are trying to build a trusting relationship and if we show great affection on a regular basis. I learned this from Asahi and her mother.

It was painful for me to hear Asahi's crying in the corridor. Every time I heard her crying, shouting to stop, not to hurt her, I interlaced my fingers and prayed that her treatment would finish soon. The reason I thought of her as a very strong child was because she never whined or gave up. She had never said, "Will I be cured?" "It's painful," "I envy other kids," or "I can't bear any more." Though she was physically weak, she was strong in spirit, so nobody felt weakness in Asahi since her will was amazingly strong. She appeared to be a god to me. She taught me that we can change health, happiness, a sense of fulfillment, and so on by having a positive attitude and positive thinking.

She always smiled and said, "I'm fine!" How many people who are experiencing such hardship can say that?

CHAPTER 3

Farewell to "the Sun"

A Found Christmas Card

On January 13, 2008, I got up in the morning and noticed an email from Asahi's mother. I wanted to read it right away, yet I was afraid of what it might say.

> Good morning. I know this is sudden, but yesterday morning Asahi's condition suddenly got worse, and she is still unconscious. Today or tomorrow will be the turning point. It is so serious that even if she recovers, she will never be as she was. I wasn't sure whether I should tell you this or not, but I found Asahi's Christmas card for you. I felt so sad that Asahi can't give this to you by herself, so I dared to email you.
>
> You are the one who makes Asahi feel better the most, besides the family. Although I did not want to bother you with this mail, I couldn't help writing. If you have time today or tomorrow, even if it's a short visit, could you please come to see her? If you came, she might want to live some more, I thought. I'm fully aware that this is a selfish request, but please excuse me.

We had never corresponded by email before and we had met only a few times at the hospital. But Asahi was so talkative—and she was so good at explaining the situation and people's feelings—that I had come to respect Asahi's mother through her. Also, her mother had sent me a New Year's card thanking me: "Asahi tells me you take very good care of her with a lot of affection, and I really appreciate you."

Luckily, through Asahi's fortuitous "mistake," her mother and I had each other's email addresses. Her mother said, "How odd it was the way we found out each other's email addresses." I agreed with her. Last December, I asked Asahi, "Your mother sent me a New Year's card last year, so I want to send her a card this year, but you moved. Can you ask your mom for her new address for me?" It was only one month before she lost consciousness.

Asahi was a smart child who seldom made mistakes, so I have no idea why she got an email address from her mother when I asked for a mailing address. When Asahi fell into unconsciousness, her mother told me, "If it wasn't for Asahi's mistake, I wouldn't have been able to ask you to come, so I feel lucky." How desperate she must have been to be told that Asahi might not make it.

She also wrote about that day in other emails. "Because of Asahi's unlikely mistake, I was able to ask you to come. Asahi had a Christmas card ready for you that I didn't know about. It was left on top of the basket where she kept her belongings so I could find it. I can't help thinking that Asahi planned all of this. She probably wanted me to call you."

We encountered other unusual coincidences in December and January. Asahi's mother was thankful we could contact each other in spite of the fact we had spoken only a few times. She was truly glad and emphasized how lucky she felt about the amazing, miraculous coincidences.

They all happened at Asahi's end. It was as if she made a picture book herself to say "farewell" so she wouldn't leave any regrets. That is how I came to receive an email from Asahi's mother on January 13. It was the one email that I didn't want to receive, the news of Asahi being in very critical condition. I didn't want to hear it, but her mother wrote, "Today or tomorrow will be the turning point." It ran through my brain. I needed to rush to the hospital.

I quickly got dressed and raced to the hospital. When I got there, I didn't hear Asahi's usual loud voice when she saw me: "Whoopee, Auntie Maeda!" Instead, there was a respiratory device around Asahi's mouth, her eyes were closed, and there was an unbelievable array of machines positioned around her tiny, thin body. It was very painful to see. Her family couldn't wait to tell her, "Asahi! Auntie Maeda is here! You've been waiting for her to come, right?" Asahi's grandparents from both sides were also there telling her that I had come. I could only imagine how sad they were.

"Asahi, are you sleeping?" I whispered.

It was painful to see her writhe in discomfort. I could hear the sorrowful sound of the medical machines in her room. Of course I knew that I wouldn't get any response, but I kept talking to her. "Please wake up and say, 'Auntie Maeda! When did you come? I didn't know you came!'"

Asahi loved being patted on her head and having her hands rubbed, but that day she had no reaction at all. She always threw herself into my arms and stayed there until I said, "Let's play!" She looked as though she was just sleeping, but I knew this time was different from before. The sound of the medical equipment sorrowfully told me how critical it was.

"She looks as if she's about to get up, doesn't she?" I said to her family. Then they remembered the Christmas card.

Towards the end of the previous year, Asahi told me, "I'm sorry I can't give you a Christmas card yet." She had vomited blood a few times in December and I knew her condition was very serious, so I told her, "Asahi, you've been very tired, so you should take it easy! No need to rush. I can wait until you feel better."

"I'll give it to you the next time I see you," she told me when I went to the hospital for the first time after the New Year. Now, it was being given to me by her family. At last I had it. I thought if I opened the envelope and saw her familiar handwriting on the card, I would shed tears, but then I remembered what Asahi said. Whenever she gave me her letters, I always asked her if I could read it then. She would tell me with her eyes sparkling, "Yes, please, now!" She was very excited and waited for my reactions. So I thought I should open the card in front of her.

There were her favorite three stickers on the red envelope. Since stickers were treasures to a child, having three stickers on the envelope was a great tribute. On the card was a Santa Claus carrying a very big bag, and above him in Asahi's handwriting, her message started with, "My heart..."

"My heart..." I wanted to know what followed next, so I quickly opened the envelope.

"...is filled with a lot of thank-yous for this year!"

Underneath these big letters were many Santa Clauses—each with a cute gift box with a different phrase written on them.

"Thank you for telling me stories."
"Thank you for playing with me."
"Thank you for being a good friend."
"Thank you for encouraging me."
"Thank you for listening to me."
"Thank you for being kind to me."
"Thank you for helping me."
"Thank you for loving me."
"Thank you for being there for me."
"I really thank you."

The inside of the card was filled with her "thank-yous." If I had been reading this card at home, the tears would have trickled down each time I read, "Thank you."

"I found the card when I was putting away her toys and belongings. She was working on this to the end," Asahi's mother said with deep thought about her daughter.

When I saw Asahi the last time, she said to me, "I haven't finished the card yet. I'm sorry." She must have been writing until just before she lost consciousness. Even her mother didn't know that Asahi finished making this card. Looking at it, I could tell how she had carefully erased and rewrote it. It was not easy for her to even use an eraser, since she was so weak and hooked up to an IV. She wrote neatly—putting her heart and soul into each letter. This Christmas card became the greatest treasure of mine—a very sorrowful but heartwarming, life-long treasure.

Asahi gave me such a wonderful card, yet I wasn't able to thank her in person. She made the card imagining how happy I would be looking at it. I was so sad looking at an unresponsive Asahi. But I couldn't shed tears in front of Asahi and her family yet. Because Asahi was still fighting to live.

I wondered when I should let Mrs. Mori—who also did volunteer work with me on Friday—know that Asahi's condition had taken a sudden turn for the worse. I was grateful to Mrs. Mori for letting me and Asahi spend so much time together. We couldn't have done so if she wasn't willing to take care of the other children in the playroom by herself.

Mrs. Mori is very kind. She had a way of communicating with children through her expressions. She had a kind of charisma that made everyone comfortable, including adults. I tried to stay in the playroom until the nurses asked me to go to Asahi's room, but Mrs. Mori always told me to go to see Asahi because she would be waiting for me. She was always thinking of Asahi and didn't mind that she would have to work harder by herself.

I therefore spent more time with Asahi than Mrs. Mori. I didn't want to burden her by letting her know about Asahi's condition, because she worked on Friday. I knew if I called her, she would definitely come in, so I hesitated to call.

Mrs. Mori used to stop by Asahi's room on her way home, and the three of us would chat, then Mrs. Mori and I would leave. Asahi sometimes wrote a thank-you letter to Mrs. Mori, for she knew her kindness. She was also concerned about Mrs. Mori's pet dog, which was getting old and weak, so she often told Mrs. Mori to take care of her dog. Mrs. Mori always admired Asahi's upbringing. It doesn't take much for kindhearted people to understand another's kindness. I think Mrs. Mori and Asahi saw through to the kindness in each other in the little time they spent together.

I finally called Mrs. Mori that evening and told her about Asahi. As I expected, she said without hesitation, "Would you come with me tomorrow?" The next day we visited Asahi in the hospital, and Mrs. Mori surprised me by talking to Asahi. "Asahi-chan, Auntie Maeda is here. I know you were waiting for her. You can tell that she is here, can't you? Hang in there." She didn't say, "Asahi-chan, I'm here, too."

What she said was exactly what Asahi's family said. Only then did I realize that although Mrs. Mori spent more time in the playroom than she did in Asahi's room, she still loved Asahi like family. If it were not for Mrs. Mori, Asahi and I could not have spent those meaningful five and a half years together. I admired her; she was the right person for volunteer work. I knew that it was very hard for Mrs. Mori to see Asahi unconscious, but I was glad I called her because I was sure her kind, warm voice definitely reached Asahi in her end.

"Guess How Much I Love You"

As it turned out, the day I saw Asahi right after New Year's was the last day we played. She already wasn't feeling very well and, although she was so young, she was keenly aware of her condition. So, when I went into her room, she couldn't decide whether to play or lie down and have me read some books.

"I want to play with you, but if I play I might get tired. I still tend to have a nosebleed, so I'm scared. I think it's better to listen to your reading."

"If we play, I might make you laugh, and, if you cough, it's not good for you. Why don't we read a book today? If you feel better next week, then we can play."

"All right! Let's read. If I play with you, I know I will laugh too much. There is a thick book my grandpa borrowed, and it's hard to read by myself, so that's the book for today! Oh, but are you able to finish reading it before you leave this morning?"

"Today is the first day this year, so I'll give you a special treat as a New Year's gift—I'll stay until I finish! You like my staying overtime, don't you?"

She didn't shout, "*Banzai!*" as she usually did when I stayed overtime. She looked so tired—I thought to myself that it was good we decided to read rather than play that day.

Just as Asahi thought, the story was too long to finish in the morning, but it was the most heartwarming story we had ever read together. It was such a wonderful book that I later thought that God had led us to read it on our last day together. She was very ill, but well enough to listen to my reading with her eyes sparkling. She loved to read.

The book was a foreign story about a blind girl who goes out to explore the woods with her friends. She might have been blind, but she could hear and smell. She had greater awareness and courage than any of her friends. She encouraged them, saying, "I can't see, but I can see through my mind. I know we will be all right passing through this road." Because of her, they succeeded in exploring woods. The girl was happy that everybody trusted her, and everybody appreciated her for leading them to a successful exploration. It was the kind of story Asahi loved.

In the story, she heard a term: "best friend." "Does 'best friend' mean a very close friend? I have friends, but I'm not sure I have a best friend. Is it okay not to have a best friend?" Asahi asked with a concerned look.

"If you have friends, you don't have to have a best friend. But you have a best friend, don't you?"

"Who is it?"

"What do you mean, 'Who?' She is right here! She is forty years older than you, but you don't mind having an older friend, do you?"

Her expression changed quickly and she asked with her eyes sparkling, "Really? Auntie is my best friend?"

"I always thought so." I smiled.

She looked happy. Reassured, she asked me to continue reading. I stayed longer than usual so I could finish reading, so she was very pleased. It was a book her grandfather had borrowed for her, but because it was a bit substantial for a child to read, Asahi wasn't able to read it herself. She had been wanting to read it for some time, so I was happy that I could read it for her.

As usual, when I was ready to leave, I said to her, "See you next week!"

She asked me shyly, "Auntie Maeda, do you know how much I care about you?" She was so cute that I can't even describe how cute she was.

"Let's see…I'm quite sure that you care a lot about me, but it's a hard question. Do you know how much I care about you, Asahi?"

"Let's play a game! A 'who loves you more?' game."

Then I thought it was a very important conversation for children. Children tend to talk to me about things, one after another, when I am getting ready to leave the hospital because they want me to stay longer. "We'll talk about it next week," I say. "Oh, that's too bad," children say. "Time's up, and I'm hungry, too. Bye-bye!" I often say so flatly, but I felt I shouldn't cut off Asahi that day. Her eyes revealed her seriousness.

"I like you so much that I want to see you more often and not only on Fridays," I said.

"I want you to be here every day!"

"I want to take you home with me because you are so darling."

"I want you to become my second mother. That's how much I love you."

"I'm thinking about you on the days when I don't come here."

Then she raised herself in bed and expanded her hands, hampered by an IV and tubes. It must have been so hard for Asahi, but she expanded both her hands as much as she could, trying to show herself much bigger than her actual self. "I love you this much. Like this. Like I jump into the space!" She tried to make full use of her will power and words.

I was moved by her expression and opened my eyes unconsciously.

"What do you think? Did I beat you or what?"

"Asahi jumps into the space! Wow, that is great!"

Children like playing games, and they want to win whatever they play, but only this game is different. She wants to win, but if she wins, it means that I love her less than she loves me. She was probably waiting for my answer with a pounding heart and eager anticipation.

"Now I was told, 'I'll jump into space,' so I have no idea now, but I won't be beaten. Asahi, do you know the phrase 'second battle'? As I was told about this game only today, I'm at a disadvantage, so will you give me a second chance next week?"

"All right, then. Does it mean this game is not settled yet?"

She looked glad, and I was relieved. I was getting ready to leave, and again Asahi spoke. "As a matter of fact, there was a picture book like this. I read it a long time ago."

"Like this?"

"The story was about which one loves the other more, or something like that, but I forgot the title of the book."

"Well, my! Is there such a cute picture book? I'm quite an expert on picture books, but I never heard of that book. I really want to read it!"

"I've read the book, but now that we're talking about it I want to read it again. I forgot the title, though, so I think it will be hard to find."

"I'll find it!"

"When you look for the book, you need the title." As she read three thousand books, she was smarter than me.

"I really want to read it with you, so I will find it! I promise! So when I do, let's read it together!"

We linked our fingers to promise, which became our last promise. I felt as if Asahi crossed her little finger tighter than ever.

The Promised Picture Book

I started looking for that picture book. One night when I was about to give up, I suddenly remembered that I had a guidebook of children's books on the night table, *Picture book guide for adults: Sixty picture books that will break your heart*. The book had sat on my nightstand for several months, but I had only scanned through it a few times. I quickly glanced through the contents and came across a title that was likely to be the picture book that Asahi spoke of—*Guess How Much I Love You?* To my regret, it was towards the very end of the catalog, where I hadn't read yet.

On the jacket was a picture of a cute little rabbit and a big rabbit facing each other. I read the summary: "I love you as much as I can reach the moon," the little rabbit said. Then I remembered what Asahi said: "I love Auntie Maeda as much as I jump into space." I remembered that Asahi said so with her eyes sparkling in spite of being so tired that day. This was the book!

I was fine until I read about the book. Then my eyes quickly filled with tears and I finally broke down crying. My husband, who was working in the same room, saw me and stopped what he was doing.

"No need to cry over a catalog of picture books. Did you find such a wonderful book that you had to cry? Did any sentence strike a responsive chord in your heart?"

I couldn't answer. Finally, I managed to say in a strained voice, "It's too late."
"What?"
"This one."
He looked at the page I pointed to and said calmly, "This is the book? Oh, you almost—"

As usual, he had very few words, but he understood exactly how I felt. Because I always told him about Asahi and me, and because he always listened, he understood right away what I meant by "It's too late." Asahi was already unconscious. Why did I miss the catalog? It had been there the whole time. I was filled with regret. I wished I had remembered it a little sooner.

I remembered Asahi, who was always listening to my reading with her eyes sparkling, and I remembered Asahi, who was unconscious and just lying on the bed. The two images appeared, alternating in my head in a flash. I would no longer be able to read this book for Asahi, as I had promised, and make her happy. I would no longer be able to look at her smiling face.

"It's too late now," my husband said. "I'm so sorry."

I could no longer control my sorrow and cried bitterly, gripping the book in my hands. "Isn't there a chance that she might regain consciousness again?"

My husband is a doctor, and he didn't want to give me an answer. After a while, he said, "You did enough. I'm sure she was happy that you took care of her."

Although I couldn't read the book for her anymore, I still wanted to deliver it in hopes that there would be a miracle.

I planned to buy the picture book the next morning and go to see her anyway. But then I got an email from her mother on my cell phone. "Asahi has just now rested in peace. I truly appreciate you."

At the moment, I understood what it meant; the memories of the five and a half years I spent with Asahi flashed through my mind. We often use an expression, "like a revolving lantern," and that is what I experienced. Scenes of Asahi and me flashed back in rapid succession. All I could do was face the facts and accept the death of an innocent nine-year-old girl. I wanted to tell her, "Asahi, I finally found it. Let's read it together." I had promised her and made her happy. That was the least I could do, but, now, it was over.

I stood in a daze, holding my phone, and thought about Asahi's mother. There isn't anything sadder to do in this world than reporting your child's death.

I thought about her and imagined that she must want to rest with her daughter. Yet she took the time to send me an email right after Asahi went to rest in eternal peace. My heart was wrung by her strength and her deepest grief.

A few months after Asahi passed away, I received an email from her mother and I came to understand a little more why she was so strong.

> I truly appreciate the doctors who never gave up on Asahi and tried their best to treat her ever since she was two years old, and especially for the last ten days while she was unconscious. I can hear Asahi saying, "You helped me so much; don't cry, everyone. I appreciate you all." That was what my family and I needed. We sincerely appreciate doctors who devoted all their energy to treat my daughter, especially during her last ten days.

For nine years, Asahi's mother was probably haunted by the fear that she might lose her dear daughter. Although she struggled, she said only grateful words in the end. I think she is very great. I think that a person's true character is tested when she or he is in the hardest situation. It's easy for us to be kind and nice when we are happy and live comfortably, but it's not easy to appreciate in the bitterest situation. I respect people like Asahi's mother. I can't be such a strong and great person. I am sure that it was Asahi who made her mother into such an appreciative person. Asahi had a power to encourage her family to the end, the family she was leaving behind. I can't find other words except admiration for Asahi.

"Don't cry, everyone. I appreciate you all." Asahi's last words her mother heard in her heart were such wonderful words, and I was encouraged, too. In the end, Asahi encouraged her mother, who had been encouraging Asahi for years. And Asahi, not even ten, taught me, almost fifty, a lot; out of all the things she had taught me, this is one moral lesson for me: "No matter how bitter your life is, accept the inevitable and appreciate the love you receive and the happiness you have."

Asahi's mother called me a few hours after Asahi passed away. "Now she is in the autopsy room."

"How sad you must be." I couldn't find words to follow. Asahi had undergone six operations. I heard she had over forty treatments by catheters. I felt very sorry that she had to be examined again when she could finally rest in peace. I felt awful thinking about how Asahi's mother must have felt. But I was so surprised by her next words: "I requested it. I asked doctors to perform the autopsy. Asahi was always happy to see her friends leave the hospital, and she was really sincere, so if she had her own will now, she would probably want to be dissected. She would want to be helpful for other friends."

Without a doubt! If she had a choice, Asahi would have requested it without hesitation. She was such a brave and warmhearted child. There's no doubt that Asahi's mother wanted to hold her daughter and take her home without a moment's delay, yet they stayed at the hospital for several more hours. Even if Asahi passed away, her mother wanted to do what her daughter would have wanted, and she tried to make it happen. Then I knew a mother's deep love and grief at the same time, and only said, "You are great!" As I hung up, I swore in my heart, *Someday I want to help her heal her grief, even a little.*

Life Like a Thread

I was often surprised at Asahi's patience, kindness, and her understanding of other people's distress. I guessed that it was probably related to her struggle against the illness. One day when I entered her room, I noticed that her friend who had shared the same room with Asahi for a long time had left, and she was playing by the empty bed by herself.

"Oh, I'm sorry. Miki-chan has left. You must feel lonely."

"Why? Good for Miki-chan; she was very happy."

Her expression was asking me, "Why do you feel sorry?" She also seemed to be complaining, "You should be happy for Miki-chan, too." I was ashamed of having a small mind. Compared to me, Asahi was great.

She was such a child that she could sincerely be happy about her friend's leaving. She was never jealous or envious, and had an amazingly tranquil mind. Perhaps because she was the one who had been waiting to overcome her illness, she had such a beautiful mind. "Congratulations! Take care!" She always blessed her friends, but her turn never came.

She could get along with anybody, endure any hardship, and make others happy. If she could miraculously go to school one day, she would fit right in without problems. I wondered how she was brought up to be such a great child.

Where and who can teach us the importance of beings? I knew of Asahi's mother's greatness, but there was another person who helped to raise her. It was Asahi's grandfather who influenced her mother a lot.

After Asahi passed away, I found that her greatness was inherited from her grandfather to her mother, and then from her mother to Asahi. "The footprints of each day naturally give the answer to life. Clear footprints hold clear water." Whenever I think about Asahi's life, I remember these words by Mr. Mitsuo Aida.

A clear and tranquil heart has been inherited by Asahi's family like a thread of spinning wheel. It is very wonderful. I want to inherit Asahi's beautiful footprint, too. I want to live so that my footprint can hold clear water, just as Asahi's did.

What is human life? If we define life as a period when we live, it depends on God, so we can't change how long we live, but I want to think that we can change the length and value of our life. Since I met Asahi, I thought about many different things—about life, illness, death, and happiness. We can weave a beautiful cloth by spinning thread carefully. In the same way, we should deal with our life, I think.

We spin thread, "my own life," in the same way we handle others' lives faithfully. If we all can do that, we will weave a big and beautiful cloth with a lot of threads.

Even if we have a long thread, one can do only so much by oneself.

"I hope that everyone handles her or his own thread, and others' thread. I hope that everyone pulls together and weaves many threads, and feels the beauty of it together."

Asahi left such a message filled with hope. Asahi, who cherished her nine-year-thread, went to heaven on January 21, 2008.

Asahi before I Knew Her

I could understand that Asahi's strength and cheerfulness could be attributed to her mother, but was still interested in the parts of her life unknown to me. I couldn't believe that her wonderful character was built only on her bed. These days, I've come to know Asahi's unknown life by exchanging emails with her mother.

Asahi and I got closer to each other when she needed to stay longer in the hospital, after she became six years old. I heard that, before then, she was pleased with W Home (an educational institution) and was given a great education there.

"When she was five, she was able to live at home for eight months, and she went to school with an almost perfect attendance," her mother said contentedly. This story proved how great W Home was and how eager Asahi was, because she had a very serious physical problem. It's easy for me to imagine how happy her mother was during that time. The eight months must have been supreme bliss for them. We sometimes complain about going to school or going to work, but I was shown our selfishness and negligence by Asahi.

Asahi attended this school since she was four. The school is intended mainly for autistic children who cannot enter regular school. There was also an institution for physically challenged children on the premises, but Asahi didn't belong to either of these groups.

Because of her serious physical condition, teachers would have to give much more care to Asahi than to other children, and most schools lack the experience of taking care of such a child. Therefore, W Home didn't accept Asahi at first. Doctors also said that it was impossible for Asahi to attend school. But thanks to Asahi's mother's hard work and W Home's solicitude, and because an acquaintance of Asahi's mother went to this school, Asahi was finally accepted.

This story was also instructive for me because I could easily choose my children's kindergarten. I had no problems because my children were healthy, but Asahi and her mother taught me that everything is worthy of appreciation.

Asahi's grandfather said, "W Home teachers looked like God. The education they offer is wonderful. It is done based on each child's ability."

Asahi's mother was so appreciative that—in spite of her very serious health issues—here Asahi was able to experience swimming, a field day, summer festival, picnic at the park, a pick-up bus, and more. She sometimes asked friends to carry her oxygen cart, and sometimes helped the driver of a pick-up bus as an assistant. At such a young age, she learned that life is a give and take: there was a time to help and a time to be helped.

When I talk about Asahi's growth, I should not only talk about her experiences at W Home, but also about the opportunities her parents and grandparents gave her. They let Asahi experience fun things—such as picking shells at the beach, playing in a snow field, dancing at a festival, catching fireflies, and so on—and she did everything with her oxygen cart and a tube. When I learned these things about Asahi, I was really surprised. When you think about Asahi's health, some of the things she was allowed to do might not have been too good for her, but if they only thought about her health and didn't let her experience anything, Asahi would not have been raised to be the strong and cheerful child that she was.

Kudos to Asahi's parents and grandparents for loving her enough to let her experience many of the challenges of everyday life, challenges she could not have experienced otherwise. Kudos to W Home's superb education as well. They raised Asahi to be a kind, strong, cheerful, and fun-loving child, and, more than anything else, they let her enjoy her life!

Asahi's final words the morning of the day she lost consciousness were, "I feel fine today, so I should practice my walking." When I heard this, I couldn't believe it. Tears welled up in my eyes because it was difficult for her just to stand those last few years. She didn't lose any hope until the end. It's a credit to her family's love that Asahi grew to be who she was. They allowed her to experience a normal life. Asahi appreciated it, and, in return, she turned their love into her own strength and energy.

After Asahi passed away, her mother sent me a pretty picture book that Asahi had made by hand, entitled *Adventures of a Polar Bear*. Asahi made it when she had to stay in the hospital for an extended period of time. She must have been so disappointed not being able to go to school, but she showed her "never give up" spirit in that book. Her picture book gave a vivid description of her feelings. Each page was filled with vigorous pictures and words. I was surprised that she made several picture books other than the one she made for her mother for her birthday. I was also very impressed that the last picture book Asahi made, *Adventures of a Polar Bear*, was so positive and engaging. She dreamed of working at hospitals, but she could have become a great writer of children's books.

The story is very childlike and cute. It is about Shiro (a white bear), a stuffed animal that had been with Asahi since she was a baby. Shiro was her favorite—a treasure that she didn't want anyone else to touch. Asahi's paternal grandmother made so many summer and winter clothes for Shiro that Asahi was very much pleased.

The way Asahi cared for Shiro was so adorable that she used to get upset with me when I picked Shiro up by his ear and handed him to her. "Don't pick him up by the ear! Hold him carefully!" said Asahi with a menacing look. She changed Shiro's clothes often and cared for him, saying, "This is my baby." She didn't ask anyone but me: "Auntie Maeda, can you pick him up and hand him to me?" That's why I think she had complete trust in me, and it's no wonder she got upset when I picked Shiro up by his ear.

I wondered what kind of adventure Asahi would have Shiro experience and looked through her picture book. The story began with Shiro going out for a walk. Shiro went to the park, enjoyed picking flowers, and went safely back home, which in itself was a great adventure for Asahi. Shiro was very happy and said, "I had a wonderful day!" and fell asleep—and that's it. It was a simple story of Shiro, with colorful pictures and full of hope. I can fully understand Asahi's mother saying, "I like this one the best because it symbolizes a positive Asahi." The end of this book was not that Shiro fell asleep satisfied, but that Shiro was excited thinking about what he would do the next day: "Well, I'm going to have another exciting day."

There was no end to Asahi's hope, even though she couldn't go to school any longer. Shiro had an adventurous day and he looked forward to having another adventurous day. I saw Asahi herself in Shiro in the book. She wouldn't give up. She would always have hope. She would have an adventure of her own, and another one, and another one. She might have had some idea about the seriousness of her illness, but her positive attitude never changed to the end. Her spirit was marvelously present in her picture book.

I understand that Asahi's mother loves this picture book in which Asahi expressed her hope the best. Asahi sent a message through Shiro and expressed her feelings brilliantly in the book. Asahi's positive view of life probably gave her mother hope. The picture book seemed to mean that Asahi hadn't given up, and her mother must have been very proud of her daughter.

I can't imagine how sad a mother is losing her child, so I thought I wouldn't be able to talk to Asahi's mother after the funeral ceremony. She probably also thought that she wouldn't see me after Asahi passed away, so when she found the Christmas card, she felt so strongly about giving it to me herself. That's why she sent me that urgent email, I suppose.

For some time I couldn't decide whether or not to let Asahi's mother know about my decision to write a book about Asahi. I suppose I lacked the courage to do so. But when the spring wind—which reminded me of Asahi—started to blow, I finally sent her an email: "I want to write a book about Asahi." She wrote me back right away and surprised me. It was a heartfelt email with kind words and her gratitude towards people who had been helpful. "I do want you to write about Asahi. I will help you as much as I can."

Thanks to her understanding, I started to write. As I wrote about Asahi, we could believe that Asahi would live forever. If it wasn't for Asahi's Christmas card, her mother and I might not have communicated, and I might not have thought about writing about Asahi.

The card told of Asahi's desire for her family to keep a relationship with me, I believe. I will keep the card as my treasure forever, and Asahi's wish in the card will be shared in her family's heart and mine. It's an invisible but supreme thing that Asahi left for us.

Everyone's Kindness

When Asahi passed away, each member of my family expressed their kindness to me in their own way.

When I first told them about starting volunteer work at the hospital, they were concerned about me. "You're going to a hospital to work with sick children? You cry so easily, you shouldn't put too much of your feeling into what you do." They made it a condition that I not put too much emotion into my work. They probably didn't want to see me crying. So I kept that in mind, but how could I have imagined such sadness?

"Mom, you must be very sad. Are you okay?" my son said in a gloomy, low voice. He shared my grief. When he read Asahi's Christmas card, he was moved to tears. He read the card that became my treasure the most courteously of all my family members. It's my son's kindness.

My daughter emailed me as soon as she heard about Asahi's death. "Asahi-chan has passed away, hasn't she? I think you were important to her. Mom, she was happy she met you. It's sad, but Asahi-chan is no longer in pain." It was a positive, refreshing email showing her personality. I could feel that gentle breeze begin to blow toward my aching heart. It's my daughter's kindness.

How often my son's kindness helped me to heal. He always sees things from my point of view. How often has my son's kindness saved me? How often has my daughter's kindness encouraged me to move toward a brighter direction? How often did her kindness show me what I needed to know?

Each of us has a different kindness. My husband has both our son's and daughter's kindness. He works hard and is extremely busy, but he always listens to my trivial conversation kindly—so much so that he could probably remember all the children in the ward.

A young man of nineteen once confided in me, "I worry whether I should marry or not because of my heart condition. If I die after we get married, I will make her unhappy. What would you do if you were me?" M-kun—he wanted to take me and his favorite stuffed animal home—ran and hugged me when he saw me when he visited the hospital as an outpatient after going home. He gave a shout of joy so loud, causing a bit of a commotion because people around us thought someone had a heart attack or something. Yūki and I played together: I played hardball with her. My husband knew all about them. So naturally he knew a lot about Asahi. When I received the email from Asahi's mother, it was my husband who took me to the hospital. "You should go right now!" I will never forget how sad he looked the day Asahi passed away. He was as sad for me as he was for Asahi. His kindness touched my heart. I will never forget it.

What I Will Treasure

The reason I never want to forget Asahi isn't that she was the most critical patient, or that she had stayed in the hospital the longest of all the children. The reason is that, coincidentally, both of us liked the words "thank you." I like people who understand gratitude.

My late father was the one who influenced me on that. He was a person who could appreciate a breezy wind. Born in the Meiji era, he was very strict, but his words left a deep impression on my early childhood. He always said, "Children are expected to appreciate their parents, pupils to appreciate their teachers, and subordinates to appreciate their bosses. One needs to do it in an opposite direction."

My old-fashioned father always said, "I'm very lucky to have such a daring child. Children make parents happy. How thankful!" After he passed away and

I had children of my own, I began to understand the meaning of appreciation. Only then did I realize that what my father told us was so full of meaning.

I complained, "It's raining, so I can't play outside." He would say, "We welcome this rain. If it doesn't rain, crops can't grow, right?" When I grumbled, "It's too hot tonight! I can't sleep," he would say, "In summer time, it should be hot. It does good for your health to be sweaty when it's supposed to be hot." Later, when I became an adult, I heard that although we were rather wealthy, we did not buy an electric fan until everyone else had one. My mother said with a dissatisfied look on her face, "Our children had heat rashes all over." I guess that my father might have been a little extreme.

His favorite saying was, "We should look on the bright side of life." One day, he pointed to a globe of the earth and told me, "When the sun shines in one country, it doesn't shine on the opposite side of the world, does it? But the sun always exists, so you shouldn't worry. You can say the same about life. We should find the bright part in our life and appreciate it. Such a person will definitely be happy."

When my father was twelve years old, he had to become an apprentice because he was the first son in a very poor family. He never felt that was unfair to him, however, and helped his parents pay the school expenses for his younger brothers. I respected my father, and his words made a deep impression on me.

I want to appreciate it when I feel a soft breeze, when I look up to the blue sky, and when I find a small wayside flower. I want to be that person. I treasure the words "thank you" as the most meaningful of all words. When I appreciate the little things, I fondly remember my father, who passed away over twenty years ago, and I appreciate his precepts.

I got married three years before my father passed away to a person who could naturally say, "Thank you," and it sounded so beautiful when he said so. Thanks to my father, perhaps, I was able to meet such a man. And now I often tell my father, silently, "Thank you, Dad. I have a happy life."

Asahi was a child who treasured "thank you" as much as my father did. No matter how sick she felt, and no matter how small a thing it was, she never forgot to say "thank you" to her friends and to the adults taking care of her.

Whenever I left her room, she said heartfelt words of gratitude—"Thank you!" after saying, "Bye-bye!" She always said so even after I left the room, and

I could hear her in the corridor. I loved to hear her voice saying, "Thank you! Please come again!"

Last Letter

Asahi loved to write and receive letters, so I put a lot of thought into what I would write in the letter that I would put in her coffin when I went to buy the stationary and the picture book I had promised her. I found just the right stationary—it featured a drawing of a bear and a dog playing in cherry petals all around them. The bear reminded me of Asahi's beloved Shiro and the dog reminded me of her pet dog, Niko. It looked like it was made just for her. I was certain she would love it.

After that I went to the bookstore, which had a stack of the cute picture books I found in the anthology. I picked up two of them because I wanted to keep one for myself. I went straight to the register, still wondering why I didn't know about such a cute picture book. When I looked at the back cover, I noticed that book was published after my children entered junior high school. *No wonder,* I thought.

I wanted to read the book immediately, but thought that it would be better to read it later—this book that Asahi wanted to read again, this book we had promised to read together—in the quiet of my home, alone.

At the counter, I was helped by a chubby, young salesman. He wore glasses and looked to be very kind. "I have many types of cute wrapping paper for children. Would you like me to wrap this with one of them?" He quickly placed several colorful sheets of wrapping paper on the counter.

"Oh, it's—" I had only thought about getting the picture book in a hurry until then, so I was at a loss for words, but managed to say, "It is for someone who passed away, so—"

"Oh, oh, I see. Let's see. Then can I give you some wrapping paper without flashy colors? Colorful ones wouldn't be appropriate."

I never heard of a rule to have a kind salesclerk for picture book sales. But to the absent-minded customer, he repeated many times, as if he were talking to himself, "I see," with a slow, soft tone. He put two books into the paper bag. It was such a healing experience for me to hear the gentle tone of his voice. I may be mistaken, but he seemed to blink his small, tender eyes inside black-framed glasses. I paid for the books and was all set, but the bag was on the counter behind the register, and he stood motionless.

"Can I have the bag?"

"Oh, I'm—I'm really sorry. I was careless. What was I thinking, not giving you what you just purchased? Thank you very much. Take care. Thank you."

He seemed to be a truly pleasant person, and his kind demeanor helped to heal my gloomy mind.

As soon as I got home, I opened the picture book.

While getting ready for bed, a sleepy little rabbit asked a big rabbit which one of them loved the other more. They went back and forth, but the little rabbit got more and more sleepy until he finally couldn't think. "I love you as much as if I can reach to the moon," he said finally, and closed his eyes. The story in the picture book didn't come to a conclusion, either.

On the last day I saw Asahi, I didn't acknowledge my defeat and left open the possibility of a second round. I left room for her to wonder if Auntie Maeda might have loved her more than she loved me. *It was a good idea*, I thought, *but, Asahi, why did you go to sleep like the little rabbit did? It is too much like the story in the book. You shouldn't have.*

It was a difficult day for me, but I felt a little warm inside because the warm-hearted picture book suited cheerful, bright Asahi very much. After closing the book, I started to write a letter.

Asahi, you battled for a long time, didn't you? You are truly great. You don't need to bear those awful treatments and painful injections anymore. You can enjoy sleeping in as long as you want to.

Thank you so much for teaching me. You have taught me a lot more than any adult has ever taught me. You have given me so many things that I can't thank you for enough: your handmade scarf, a beaded necklace that you devoted two days to making, your handmade charm, which you made with your favorite colored folding paper, your handmade "origami" sandwich that you made during your lunch time, your letters, your precious photos...

I couldn't help crying when I saw all of those "thank-yous" in your last Christmas card. Besides these physical gifts, you have also given me many intangible gifts to treasure. Thank you.

"What intangible gifts?" you might ask. So I have decided to thank you every year when you become ten, eleven, twenty, thirty, and forever.

Remember the picture book we promised to read together on the last day I visited you? I found it the night before you went to heaven. I had been looking for that book, and I was so sad because I didn't find it before you left us.

You had always complimented me by saying, "I enjoy when you read to me a hundred times more than when others read." Yet I found the book too late, so I couldn't read it for you. I am so sorry.

Remember the day you asked me, "Do you know how much I care about you?" We compared which one of us cared for the other more, didn't we? Although you had a hard time moving your hands because of the IV, you managed to expand both your hands, and told me, "I love you as much as if I can jump into space." Remember? Your eyes shined that day the same way they shined when you were fine, and I was very glad for you.

Then you tried to remember the name of the picture book. "As a matter of fact, there is a picture book in which the characters compare how much they love the other. I'm so sorry that I forgot its name. *How Much Do I Love?* or something like that."

"I really want to read the picture book," I told you, and you said, "Me, too!" "Okay, I'll find it, so when I find it, let's read it together." I'm very sorry that this promise became our last one.

Asahi, the rabbit in the picture book actually said, "I love you as much as if I can reach to the moon," not "jump into space," as you had guessed, but I thank you for coming up with such a great expression: "jump into space." I was happy to read the picture book because it was such a warmhearted story. But it reminded me of so much of your spirit that I cried and cried because I wanted to read it in the special way just for you.

The picture book's name is *Guess How Much I Love You*. Because you had a good memory, I could find it.

It's really important for us to pass our love to the people that we love. You had many people whom you loved, so you remembered about the picture book you read when you were really small, and you wanted to read it again, right? You'll definitely continue to live in their hearts.

And you won't be needing all of those medical instruments this time around. You can enjoy running around like you always wanted to. You can eat as much ice cream and drink as much juice as you want. You can do everything and shout with that joyful voice of yours, "Whoopee!"

Whenever you saw me, you called out loudly from your bed, "Auntie Maeda!"

Luckily, on the day we saw each other for the last time, we swore to each other. We said, "You and I are forty years apart in ages, but we are great friends to each other."

I'll treasure the memories I shared with you since you were three years old. You were sick and you were so young, but you always worried about your mother. But you don't need to worry about her any longer. She is much greater than I imagined, and she has started to walk the path of her life. She knows your wish very well and doesn't want you to worry about her, so she acts courageously. So you can feel relieved and live comfortably in heaven with many warmhearted friends.

I will also try hard not to feel so beaten, so please watch over me. "It's funny for you to rely on me because you're forty years older than me," I can hear you say in your usual cheerful Osaka dialect. You were greater than any adult, and the substance in your life was much more than nine years, I believe. We all appreciate you. Thank you for giving us so much strength.

You have a wonderful name, and I often asked you, "Who named you 'Asahi'?"

In the morning, the sun rises powerfully into the sky, becoming brighter as it rises. The sun never neglects its duty, and shines on all the people around the world alike and heats the globe.

We all need the sun. Even if we feel grief in the dark night, we can face tomorrow because the sun will rise again in the morning and the sun will encourage us.

You are kind and strong, just like the sun you were named after. Every morning, people all over the world will look up into the sky and greet you, "Thank you! I'm pleased to meet you again." We'll be together always.

January 23, 2008

I wrote the letter to Asahi on the cute stationary that matched her very well, using some *kanji* (Chinese characters) that I knew she would know, and the rest in Japanese Hiragana. When I was done, I emailed her mother:

> Asahi must be happy to finally come home. I'll visit her tomorrow. I'll visit her not to say goodbye, but to welcome her back into our lives, in our hearts from now on.
>
> Will you say hello to her from me for now and tell her, "You can see Auntie Maeda every day from now on—not just on Friday"? I will come tomorrow a little before noon and bring our promised picture book and my letter to her. I wrote to her in my letter, "People all over the world will look up at the sky and greet you every morning and appreciate you."
>
> I will never, ever forget her—not even one day. I deeply sympathize with your family and I'm worried about your health. I beg your pardon that I pass my feeling by email.

As soon as we met the next day at the ceremony, Asahi's mother told me, "Yesterday, we all cried reading your email. You made us feel better. Thanks to you, we could hold today's funeral with a sense of peace. My father appreciated it very much and told me to save your email."

Then I felt that I could fulfill my wish to heal her grief as much as I could when I hung up the phone, shedding tears that day.

A Rooter's Song for Tomorrow

The hall in which we saw Asahi off was brand new and very clean. I was determined not to cry that day because tears did not suit Asahi, who was just like the sun. My determination wavered as I approached the reception area, however, and I noticed that the receptionists' faces were already tearful.

The ceremony room was well lighted and Asahi, in a photo, was smiling, surrounded by lots of flowers, stuffed animals, and so on. The melody of "Totoro Music Box" played much more slowly and tenderly than what we heard in the movie. I was surprised to hear the melody I liked so much.

"Asahi, once I hear my favorite song on such a sad day, I won't be able to listen to this melody from now on because it will make me feel sad," I murmured in my heart. But then I could hear Asahi say in her cheerful Osaka dialect, "What are you talking about? This is a rooter's song for me to go to heaven, right? You should love this song." I felt that she cheerfully patted me on the shoulder saying so.

Asahi's mother acted courageously, bowing to the mourners and reminiscing with them as usual. I don't have words to explain her strong attitude. If I were her, I probably would not have been able to stand by myself. She saw me and walked toward me.

"Thank you very much for coming. Asahi is resting in peace and she looks great, so please take a look."

I bowed very low and approached her coffin. I looked at Asahi and wondered what I should say to her. There was so much that I wanted to say, but once I started to talk, I wanted to cry. "She was released from everything."

"Yes, she looks so comfortable, doesn't she? No more IV and respirator and such. I think she definitely waited for your coming the most."

Her sleeping face was very beautiful without swelling or signs of the struggles she showed several days ago.

I saw Asahi for the first time without an oxygen inhaler, a portable electrocardiogram, and IV. Finally, she was set free, and I was sorry that she couldn't run around. How I wished she could run around as she pleased. Even if it was only once, I wanted her to do everything she wanted to do.

My feelings were torn as I looked at Asahi in her tiny coffin. I was happy to see her released from all the hardship, but it bothered me that she couldn't run around. The two feelings intermingled; it was beyond description.

Asahi's favorite stuffed animal, Shiro, which she treasured the most next to her own life, was snuggled on her left side. Kindhearted Asahi would lend any of her toys to her friends except Shiro. He was like her soul mate, and she always took him everywhere—especially to the operating room and examination room. Shiro stayed with Asahi on days when she felt lonely because her mother wasn't there, on the anxiety-filled nights before a terrible examination. Shiro stayed with her all the time since Asahi was a baby. Shiro had stayed with her much longer than her mother and was her treasure, and he was snuggled right next to her. I remembered the last Halloween party at the playroom the previous autumn. Asahi made a wonderful costume for Shiro with folding papers and was full of spirit that she would attend the party with him. Her eyes sparkled with excitement.

I was happy to see the three toy dogs we played with in the last few months of her life. They were made of felt and put to her right side. They were very cute, and Asahi loved to play house with them and gave names to each of them.

"Asahi, your mom knew about our playing with these dogs, didn't she? She knew that we laughed like crazy, so she put them in here for you."

"Why wouldn't she? They mean a lot to me. These are the ones I played with with you. What would I do without them?"

"That's true. You and I have more to play with them… Asahi, don't forget that I'm the one who made you laugh like crazy. All right?"

"How can I forget? You made me laugh so much that I almost choked."

Watching her face, I could talk to her forever. Because I had arrived early, there was more time for me to stay with Asahi, but I finished visiting her and gave her mother my letter and the picture book I promised to bring. I was heartbroken to think that after this parting I would never see her again.

I wanted to put her mother's feelings ahead of mine, so I said, "If you read this letter and there's no problem, please put it in her coffin. It's sealed, but I brought a photocopy of it in case you might want to know the content."

Asahi's mother smiled and said firmly, "How thoughtful of you, but I want Asahi to read it first. I would never check the letter you wrote to her. I look forward to reading it after Asahi."

How courageous she can be! She was so strong to be able to leave everything up to her daughter. She never treated Asahi like a sick person, and raised her to be like the sun she was. I was so impressed to see Asahi's mother's strength even at her daughter's funeral.

In a short while, the ceremony started. The emcee calmly and slowly read a telegram from Asahi's teacher.

"'Teacher, don't cry, all right?' I heard you say this in your cheerful Osaka dialect, Asahi."

Listening to the condolatory telegram, I thought we all had the same feeling. Every time we remember Asahi, we think of her as a cheerful, happy-go-lucky girl. That image of her prevailed over the grief that we felt.

"She gave us strength until the end. She was definitely such a high-spirited girl. No matter how hard her day was, she always had more cheerful energy about her. What a wonderful girl she was."

"Totoro's Melody," which played during the ceremony, was not a sad melody for me any longer.

The ceremony concluded with Asahi's grandfather, who was the chief mourner. To think about how he must have felt to be the chief mourner of his granddaughter was too much for me. Of course, his eyes were wet with tears, but it was a great address. It was an address made by someone who had raised Asahi's wonderful mother.

Just then, what I had imagined through Asahi was proven right in front of me. Her grandfather praised Asahi for living her life cheerfully, even if it was for only nine years. He expressed words of gratitude to the people who had come to know his granddaughter during those nine years—her hospital, elementary school, friends, and so on. He didn't break down crying, wasn't upset, and politely thanked everyone with the warmhearted tone of his voice. He didn't express any of his complicated and unbearable feelings that must have recurred in his mind. His address—so full of gratitude and appreciation—transformed a sad ceremony into a bright one, and it suited Asahi, who was like the sun.

Whenever I used to say to Asahi, "Your mom and grandpa are great people, aren't they?" Asahi would ask, "How do you know that? You've only met them a few times." So I spoke to Asahi in the picture in my heart, "Asahi, I was right. They are as great as I expected, right?"

The emcee said, "The time to say goodbye has come. Everybody, please approach the coffin and pay floral tributes."

Even the emcee, who was stout and over six feet tall, had teary eyes, too. I told myself it was time to say "thank you" clearly.

"Asahi-chan, in heaven you can play as much as you want. Please enjoy everything you couldn't do while you were here. You can go in the swimming pool! You can eat anything you want!" I heard the voices of young mothers. They might have been the mothers of Asahi's friends from the hospital. I couldn't look at the people surrounding me.

"Asahi, thank you so much. I really appreciate you." I was able to thank her. Although I had patted her on the head many times, I did it again for the last time, and I praised her in my heart, "You are truly great!"

We continued to speak to Asahi, and many encouraging words continued.

"Asahi, don't feel alone. We are all here."

The moment I spoke to her for the second time, people around me suddenly began to cry loudly. Probably everybody had felt the same as me.

For all the years at the hospital, I thought I was the one trying to encourage Asahi and trying to make her happy, but now I realized it was me who felt alone. I told her not to feel alone, but she didn't even look like she felt alone. I was the one who felt alone as my very precious friend was about to leave.

"Now, it is time for her family members to say goodbye, so can everyone else please go down to the lobby on the first floor?" At the emcee's prompting, we all went down to the first floor and watched the family's final farewells on a TV monitor. Everyone's eyes were filled with tears.

Asahi's mother patted Asahi on the head many times and left, only to return again. She repeated it. She simply couldn't resign herself. Even if she tried to leave many times, she couldn't help but to return. Like her father, she had been calm, but apparently she wasn't ready to leave Asahi yet.

She had always been strong in any situation, so to see her unable to leave her daughter at the very end was that much more meaningful for me. She was just a mother who didn't want to leave her daughter, and the mother's love for her daughter affected me so much.

"Asahi, you are very lucky because you were born to a great mother, yeah?" Asahi and her mother taught me so much more than I can even describe.

When we stepped outside, the steady rain, which had been falling all morning, stopped, and the sun shone over us.

I prayed with my hands together and bowed deeply to the hearse. After that, on the way to the station, I heard someone calling me from afar. The voice gradually got louder and louder. I looked back.

"Auntie Maeda! Thank you so-o-o much! Please come again! Thank you!"

That is what Asahi always said every time I left her room. The voice sounded louder and more cheerful than at any other time I could recall. It was as if she were trying to encourage me on my lonely journey home alone. Asahi's "thank-yous," filled with kindness, echoed in my ears and filled my heart—forever.

この一年の ありがとうの気持ちでいっぱい！
いろんな話を聞かせてくれてありがとう
一緒に遊んでくれてありがとう
なかよくしてくれてありがとう
やさしくしてくれてありがとう
はげましてくれてありがとう
助けてくれてありがとう
ありがとう
話を聞いてくれてありがとう
ありがとう
かわいがってくれてありがとう
ありがとう
ほんとにありがとう
そばにいてくれてありがとう
前田さんへ
今年もありがとう
ございました。らい年も
よろしくね
朝ひより
MERRY CHRISTMAS

APPENDIX

——— Asahi's Grandpa, "Ji-ji" ———

Leader of Asahi's Support Team

Rooting

Right after Asahi was born with a serious heart problem, I became a leader of her support team. My goal was, first, to support my daughter, and then to help her raise her daughter. I believed that if her parents were to give their best, their child could be brought up fine. We, as grandparents, needed to assist Asahi's parents so that they could care for Asahi. Such was our duty, I believed, so we acted on it.

Asahi and her parents moved into our neighborhood when Asahi was a year and a half old. In those days, she loved to ride her favorite toy vehicle, the "Anpanman" car. When she was three, Asahi could ride a bicycle with training wheels. She could go up and down the stairs in her house by herself. She walked to her house in the evening, looking up at the night sky.

I often took Asahi outside. "Being handicapped is part of who she is," I believed. I took her everywhere I could—to the *bon* dance (Japanese cultural festival which is originally a religious ceremony), field day, festivals, and so on. We went to the park and to a hillside to see nature. We walked around town, and Asahi began to love having people around her. While she struggled against her illness, she appreciated the slightest freedom she could get. She looked forward to going out and coming home for a short visit from the hospital. Asahi's parents and I gave a lot of thought as to how we could help Asahi live her life to the fullest within her limitations. I tried anything I could think of. I read her books and taught her proverbs such as, "It's like water off a duck's back." She enjoyed playing cards and was very good at it. She was quick to absorb any new knowledge. She enjoyed everything.

When Asahi was feeling well, I took her out. One day we picked flowers in the park, and she was so engaged in picking flowers. She went home holding a big bunch of flowers and told her mother, "This is for you!" Her voice was full of excitement. In this way, she enjoyed every minute of every hour of every day, and her range of activities expanded.

Asahi's life circle started to grow as she grew—neighbors, schools, the hospital—and she was quick to adapt to her surroundings. Many people Asahi met became a part of her support team. They watched over her and cared for her. Because of them, she was able to live her life happily.

Grandpa's Visit to the Hospital

We scheduled our visits to see Asahi in the hospital so she wouldn't feel so lonely. Her mother went on Tuesday, Thursday, Saturday, and Sunday. I went to see her on Monday, leaving my office at five, arriving at the hospital at 5:45. When I got to her room, she was usually playing by herself.

"Hi, Asahi."

"Hi, Ji-Ji! What did you bring for me today?"

"Guess what?"

"*Takoyaki* (ball-shaped octopus dumpling)*!*"

"Bingo!"

"Is that it?"

"No, I have more."

"Well, an egg?"

We committed small offenses against the hospital's dietary restrictions for Asahi. When Asahi was through eating, the first thing we usually did was read. Sometimes she asked, "Ji-Ji, what do you want to play?"

"Cards!"

We were pals. We enjoyed playing games, folding papers, drawing pictures, and, when she was feeling fine, we explored in the hospital. My two-hour visits went by so quickly. I tried to be nonchalant when I left her. I didn't want to remind her that she was seriously ill.

"Goodnight!"

"Goodnight!"

"I'll come again."

"Please come again!"

"See you, bye-bye."

"Bye-bye!"

Asahi and Ji-Ji at Tsurumi-Ryokuchi Park

Tsurumi-Ryokuchi Park is the most memorable place for Asahi and me. We used to go there on Saturdays whenever Asahi made one of her rare visits home. I looked forward to those occasions. I would call her house in the morning to see if she was up. "No, still sleeping," I would often be told. Both of her parents work, so they stayed up late. Asahi's mother would wake her up and ask, "Ji-Ji's on the phone. He is asking if you want to go out or not. Do you want to go?" Asahi answered loudly, "Of course!" We started doing this when she was about three years old and continued until she was about eight.

We used to go to the park by bicycle, looking at flowers all over the wayside. We would ride pass the W School, which Asahi had attended since she was four. She was able to receive a wonderful education in the small-class setting she needed. The teachers seemed like gods to me.

Whenever we stopped by, the teachers kindly talked to Asahi: "Where are you going? How nice...I wish I were going with you."

"No, you can't! I'm going with Ji-Ji!"

We went to the park often in the spring and summer when the weather was good. We looked at the horses at an equestrian club. Asahi would say, "That girl is a good rider, isn't she? When I'm older, I wonder if I can ride that well."

I let her go in the stream in the children's wood. She would go barefooted. She enjoyed the slide and the swing, the rocking horse, and so on. She had so much fun.

We sometimes stopped at a concession stand. "What do you like to eat?" I would ask Asahi. Sometimes she wanted *takoyaki*, sometimes she wanted jumbo sausage, and we always shared an ice cream cone.

Compact cars named the "Salvia" and the "Tulip" run around the mountain area in the park, and Asahi liked them very much. People with handicaps and senior citizens were given priority to ride them, so Asahi could always get in first. She enjoyed the twenty-minute ride, looking at peach branches, plums, tulips, roses, hydrangeas, salvias, cosmos, and so on, with me next to her. The drivers also served as guides. Talkative Asahi would make friends with them and ask, "What is that flower?" The driver would tell her, and Asahi would enjoy looking at the flowers twice as much.

One day she asked to ride the "Tulip." On the car, her head turned rhythmically from right to left with the music. I often heard that song, but I still don't know what the title is.

Next, we walked toward the pond where the ducks and turtles were. By the pond were a lot of pigeons and someone was feeding them. Asahi liked pigeons, so she chased them and played with them. I let her sit in the shade, and she picked flowers around her. I did the same a little farther down and returned to her and gave her the flowers I had picked. We picked a lot of flowers—yellow ones, red ones, purple ones, and white ones—and put them in the basket of our bicycle. She was on a mission to find a four-leaf clover and finally found one. "Ji-Ji, I found one!" shouted Asahi. Now, her mother keeps this four-leaf clover as her treasure.

We used to go all over the park—the exercise area, the Children's Wood—riding our bike, and listening to the sound of the stream. The park was our home base, and the memories are indeed precious ones.

A Stroll with Asahi

Sometimes, Asahi could come home for a longer visit. One such occasion, after coming home from work, I usually found Asahi playing by herself. The days were longer in the summer. "Asahi, do you want to take a walk with me?" She would answer right away, "Yes, yes!" I would put an oxygen inhaler on our bicycle rear carrier and, with Asahi in front of me, we would set out on our familiar course.

We went straight past the supermarket, then up a short hill. "Heave-ho!" Knowing exactly what I would say, she would say it before I did. She was excited to see everything. "A police car! A fire engine!" When we got to the park, she would look for a black cat that she was afraid of. "Is he going to be here? Good! I don't see him today." Happy, she would start to play on the slide. While out for a walk, we sometimes bumped into my friends, so we would stop to talk for a while. Then we visited my friend's house. He let us feed his carp. The family always welcomed us and we talked. Asahi loved to talk.

"Next, I want to visit a swimming school," she said. They had two tropical fish tanks there, and Asahi kept busy looking at the fish, going back and forth between the two tanks. She watched children swimming in the pool, too. "That girl is good at swimming. I wonder if I could swim like her when I get big like her."

When Asahi was four, we went out for a walk at night. "Look how beautiful the moon is! It's a full moon. Really, it is!" We walked some more. I told her, "The moon took a liking to you. She follows you around."

"Oh, she really is. She must like me!" Asahi looked very happy.

On another occasion, as we walked in the rain, I told Asahi, "Look, it's raining. The rain is thunder's pee."

"Hmm, the thunder is taking a long wee-wee, isn't it?"

Later, one day she asked, "Ji-Ji, is today's thunder a child? Not a whole lot of pee." She had me stumped.

Asahi, Can You Hear Me?

When you were born, we worried about you. Even if you couldn't exercise, we wanted you to find something you liked to do. If you were a healthy, normal baby, we could take our time raising you, but you only had such little time. We wanted you to live your life to the fullest. If it was something we thought you liked, we let you do it—and we let you do many things.

In the hospital, your mother and doctors fought hard for you. You probably didn't know that sometimes your mother was so tired from fighting for you, did you? She always pretended to be fine in front of you, so you could rely on her. Mom was your favorite person in the whole world.

One day she had a cold and had a fever, but she went to see you anyway. Then she called me, "Ji-Ji, I feel sick. Please come help me." I rushed to the hospital and helped her to lie down on the sofa in the lobby, then went to see you in your room. When you heard about what happened, you wanted to go see her right away. "Mom, are you all right? I hope you'll be fine soon." You wanted her to go home. You were so kind. I remember the time I was tired, too. When I asked you to let me lie down for a while, you were worried about me. It made me feel good that you worried about me.

You once called me "Dad." And you said, "Whoops, my mistake." I'm not your dad, but I think of myself as a second father because I'm a leader of your cheering section. We had dinner together in the hospital, read books together, and played together. It was a lot of fun. Do you remember what I told you a long time ago? "Aren't you lucky to have four houses? Yours, Ba-ba and mine's, your dad's parents', and the hospital." Do you remember? No matter where you were, you were loved and accepted. You got to know everyone, and you enjoyed their company. You are great! I'm so proud of you.

We didn't think you could attend elementary school, but you did, and we were all so moved. It was very interesting when you had an interview at the school. You were so excited and sat down on the sofa with vigor, so you sank back deep into the sofa. And you looked to be acting bigger than the principal. I was glad you made a lot of friends at the school.

Your going out and coming home for a visit were limited, but we played a lot together, didn't we? I remember well. We promised that we would go to Oita Prefecture to see Taro (a dog) if you could leave the hospital, didn't we? How I wish I could take you there just one more time.

Asahi, you were a great child to always be so positive. Your strength came from your belief in yourself. "Try hard; anything is possible." Asahi, your body wasn't healthy, but your sprit was so extraordinary and strong. You were kind and cheerful. I'll give you A+. Although you had a lot of restrictions, you had a lot of things you liked to do—handcrafts and reading books. I borrowed many books from the library for you, and you started to read more and more. It wasn't easy to borrow and carry twenty books per week, but I enjoyed reading children's books with you.

Though you had to stay in the hospital for a long time, you always said, "I'm busy every day!" Now I know what you meant. You had a lot of things to do for yourself and think about your support team, didn't you? When I told you that I would retire the following year, you were happy, weren't you? I've finally retired. I will be working part-time for a while, but now I have some time for myself. I'm not as busy as you were because I don't have many things I want to do, like you did. So I should find things to do and keep myself busy. I read when I fail in something.

Now, I feel alone because you are not here. But along with your mom (your favorite person) and Ba-ba, and other people in your support team, I shall follow in your footsteps to your wonderful world filled with kindness.

I showered you with my love, Asahi. And, in return, you gave me even more love. A million thank-yous!

"Dear Asahi"

Letter from Mom

Dear Asahi,

You did great! I am so proud of you. I shall draw many circled flowers on your head with my forefinger like I used to when you wanted me to praise you. I can hear you laughing and saying, "Stop, you're messing up my hair!"

You once asked me why we named you "Asahi." Since you were in my womb, we already knew that you would be born with a heart problem. When we were thinking about what to name you, your dad was looking through a name book and asked me, "How about this?" The name he found was "Asahi," which means "the morning sun" in Japanese. It was the perfect name for you. The morning sun rises, shines, and gives us hope. I could take no other name but Asahi. You should be getting well with this name. You did rise. You did grow to be a joyful child, just like the morning sun we named you after.

It was funny visiting shrines with you at New Year's. While we all prayed for you to get well, ever since you were two you always prayed for a puppy. Your wish finally came true shortly after you had a critical surgery when you were seven. Your grandma Ba-ba got you a puppy, Niko. Niko thinks of you as his mom. As he had never come to your bed upstairs before, it was startling that he showed up in your room on his own when you came home cold and small. We were all so surprised. Now, we all take good care of Niko like we did of you; and, in return, he makes us smile whenever we call him, "Niko, Niko" (smiley), just as you named him. We are glad to have him with us. He is a precious gift to us from you.

I owe you many more thanks. Thank you for believing in me when I told you the single most important lie of my life, "Try hard, and you'll get well." "Was it a lie?" you might ask. Please don't be upset. Since you believed in what I said, I was able to believe it myself, too. I could believe that such a thing would come true. Therefore, I was able to fight for you and fight alongside you.

I thought it came true when we took you to Tokyo Disneyland when you were three. You didn't know this, but everyone had told us it wouldn't be possible. Because you needed an oxygen bottle and one bottle lasts only three hours, we always drove a car when we went out with you. If we took a bullet train to go to Tokyo, we needed to take at least three bottles besides our change of clothes and stuff. Flying was even harder because of the complex procedures and tough regulations to carry oxygen bottles on board. So, we had no other choice but to drive. "It takes ten hours to go to Tokyo by car," people said. "Asahi is not strong enough, so it's not possible."

To tell you the truth, doctors had informed us earlier that they wouldn't be able to give you treatments any longer and that it would be all up to you if you wanted to live or not. That was the very reason we decided to take you to Disneyland.

I spoke to your primary doctor when you weren't around. "Wouldn't she be more enthusiastic if she knew that she could have more fun like this if she stays alive?" And, with those words, he finally gave us permission. Not only did the doctor give us permission, he was also very cooperative in searching for cardio-vascular clinics near Disneyland and writing a detailed, seven-page referral to explain your medications and your condition just in case.

Just as I hoped, after our trip to Disneyland, the more we went out, the more you wanted to go out.

"Where are we going next?"

"I heard they are going to have the animation characters' show at a certain amusement park. Can you take me to that show when I get well or when I come home for a visit?"

"My favorite animation will be released soon."

You wanted to go back to Disneyland again, and so we did.

When your condition started taking a turn for the worse, your doctor told you, "You may go home for a visit, but you can't go out." You told him, "There is no sense for me to go home if I just stay home and do nothing. I'll be good and wear a mask, so can I go out just for a while?"

You surprised me with the way you lived your life, which is just as I had wished for you. That is why I decided not to go easy on you. If I did, you might not have tried to live your life as bravely as you did.

I never once "went easy" on you—not even when we played cards. You wanted to play one more every time you lost, and you got better and better until you finally beat me with a big grin on your face. I was so serious that I hated to admit my loss. Because I played for real, you played for real. As I believed in that, I also tried to give you as much information as I could about your treatments. You accepted them, and, once you determined and made a promise, you kept your word and never ran away. I couldn't be more proud of you. I was sure that no one could have been stronger than you.

Your doctors were afraid that you were vulnerable to infection, so they told you to wear a mask when you went out. The mask became as important as the oxygen tank in your life. You always wore a mask—even just to leave your room. And when you couldn't find your mask, oh, boy! You made a big fuss! I also remember you saying, "If I had a mask on, I can go out, right?" It was so like you to say that.

I can tell you now how I felt when you had to have a catheter treatment. I pretended it was not a big deal, saying, "Don't worry, it's going to be done quickly. Just go, and I will see you soon here." I knew it might not be appropriate to say that, smiling, when you were going to have the treatment at the risk of your life. However, I was determined not to cry or feel sad in front of you because you needed me to be strong, and I knew you would be at ease if I did not appear worried.

I remember one day when you were about four. On the day before the treatment, while people were telling you, "Give it your all," you suddenly started crying. I asked you why you were crying because you had been fine before. You told me, "I hate people telling me to give it my all. I have already done all I could. How can I try any harder?" Then you cried hard. I'd never known it was such a harsh thing to say, "Give it your all."

After that incident, I was careful not to say that phrase to you. Instead, I would say, "See you soon!" And I realized that you also tried not to say those words to your friends. I was impressed by what you said to your friends when you heard they were about to have an operation: "As I have had many operations myself," you said, "I can tell you that you don't need to worry. All you have to do is sleep." I was surprised to hear that from you, who had always cried before any operations. It was so nice of you.

I always told you not to cry unless you were sick or in pain, but I did cry alone at home when I had to decide for you to have a catheter treatment. I told myself what I told you, "It doesn't help to cry over a situation that you are not able to change." Asahi, you would be upset. "What? You were crying, too?" But do you remember I also told you that I was a crybaby? You looked surprised, yet also a little relieved and happy. Since that time, every time when we watched a sad scene in a TV show, you looked into my face and said, "You are crying again, aren't you?"

You were always concerned about me, as if you had been my mother. Because I was so forgetful, whenever I was about to leave your room at the hospital, you used to tell me, "Do you have everything with you? Take care. Let me know if you got home all right next time you visit me."

When you were going to the care center, the director of the center said that she didn't feel like she was talking to a child. The way you talked was like an adult—that of a middle-aged woman in Osaka, to be more specific, as you were so straight and funny. You enjoyed being called that. While looking for good pictures of you for this book, the memoir Auntie Maeda wrote about you, I found you had smiled most at the center. You must have had a lot of fun there. I'm so glad you were able to go to that center. Also, from the pictures taken of you then, you were probably in the best condition back then. In other pictures taken later, you looked a little tired.

After you entered the elementary school, you unfortunately had to spend most of the time in the hospital. But it was good we had permission from the hospital to attend the entrance ceremony. Two months later, when you were able to go back to school, everyone remembered you. Although you went to school for just a short period of time, you made a lot of friends. They came to our home and played with you. You were so happy. Some of them still come to see you. Aren't you glad?

You couldn't go to school, but you had a teacher from the special education program come to the hospital three times a week. Although you said you didn't like to study, you looked happy talking about what you learned. Watching your condition, the teacher played games and taught you as you would like—music and art as well. When you heard that you would sing at the special education school's cultural festival, or that a special education teacher would accompany you to attend the music competition in the elementary school, you were so excited. "When the instrument and the song are chosen, I will learn how to play them." You told me I must come see you at those events. After all, I'm sorry that you couldn't perform at those events, but your teacher recorded you singing at your music lesson and gave the tape to me. I listened to it the other day. I flipped out that you could sing in such a high-pitched voice. I knew how you sang in karaoke. In the tape you sounded so different, so serious. If I told you that I thought it was funny that it didn't sound like you at all, will you be mad?

I found that I wasn't the only one you scolded. I learned that when you lost consciousness for ten days after vomiting blood, the doctors and nurses who were taking care of you, wiping your body and providing you the aspiration, were all talking about "words of Asahi." "Oh, what are we doing here? Asahi is going to scold us. She would say, 'Ouch! You're all thumbs!'" That made me aware that you scolded them, too. But they also praised you, and said that you always thanked them at the end.

Asahi, were you listening to what they were saying? Do you remember that day?

You always became a monster due to anesthesia for catheterization, as you did on the day after the catheter treatment. You made a big fuss about taking off hemostatic seals by yourself because it hurt when others did it. You were crying because it still hurt even if you did it yourself. You couldn't take the last seal off, and the nurse asked if you wanted her help with it. Then you answered politely, "Yes, please. Thank you, ma'am." Up until that time, you were yelling and crying, "Hey, stop. I'm doing it myself because you don't know how!" We all laughed so hard.

As you had so many catheter treatments, anesthesia didn't work as well as it did before. As a result, they had to give you more anesthesia over time, and it took longer for you to awaken. After the treatments, towards the end of your life, you were a monster for a while, and doctors and nurses had such a hard time with you. As you came awake, however, and maybe because you were still dizzy from anesthesia, you always politely thanked everyone. To hear you speak so politely made us all laugh.

So, during the last ten days, we all spoke to you. "Asahi, get mad and wake up!" Especially that doctor—you could tell she was coming from her footsteps, and you used to argue with her all the time in your loudest voice. Every time someone told you to wake up, your low blood pressure suddenly went up. We were sure you could hear us. Did you hear us? I believed so. I thought I heard you thanking everyone. Was I right?

I also heard you telling me not to cry. I will do my best not to cry, so I won't be scolded by you. You told me "thank you" many, many times. But, let me say,

"Thank *you*, Asahi." You are still my precious Asahi, and you will be forever. I'm glad I had you. These nine years we spent together was the happiest time. You brought me a great deal of happiness, Asahi. A million thank-yous.

Love,

Your Mom

EPILOGUE

I didn't set out to write a journal of Asahi's life in the hospital. That was never my intention. Asahi battled her illness for a long time, yet I never felt an ounce of darkness in her to the end. Asahi, the sun, was a creation of the wonderful work of her mother, who raised her with great spirits. Asahi's mother taught her the importance of life and relationships we need in our lives. She taught Asahi to never lose sight of her values in her fierce battle with her illness. She succeeded in passing those values to Asahi, so I believe that her "sun" hasn't set.

I will be talking to Asahi for years to come. Whenever I see beautiful things or am having fun, I will talk to her so she can feel what I feel. She will live in a special spot in my heart, I believe.

I went to the funeral ceremony but couldn't go to the wake. Later, I learned that four hundred and fifty people went to the viewing to see Asahi. The impressive thing is that these people actually knew Asahi and were not just acquaintances. This is an amazing number for a nine-year-old child.

When Asahi's mother told me how many people attended the vigil, it reminded me of what a delightful child Asahi was, never wasting time and always making people happy. "Asahi was only able to attend elementary school for a month and a half, but because she was so outgoing, she made a lot of friends—from school, preschool, the hospital, and many neighbors—and they all came to see her. I appreciate that Asahi can live in so many people's hearts."

Asahi was born in a hospital, spent most of her life there, and passed away in the same hospital. Enduring such hardship, she touched so many people's hearts. There is no doubt that she was an admirable child who lived a beautiful life.

Now, Asahi's mother tries hard to go on with her life. She returned to work just a week after the funeral ceremony. I was so impressed with her email. "I dispel my melancholy mood and work hard so Asahi won't scold me." She didn't lose Asahi. On the contrary, Asahi was released from her illness, and I believe her healthy soul gives her mother strength and they live on together.

Now, I can calmly remember that little girl who always wished for her mother's happiness the most. I pray that Asahi's life will continue without losing its luster, protected in her mother's heart.

I met Asahi's mother only a few times at the hospital, and later, as I learned more about her, I felt embarrassed for trying to write about her and Asahi. I mean, I felt I'd been a little haughty because I realized that their greatness was beyond my descriptive capability. But I remembered the kindness and support I received from many people. More than anything else, I remembered how Asahi's family awaited my book these past months, so I decided to go ahead and publish this book as I had planned.

If such a great child had lived longer, what kind of adult would she have become? How many people would she have touched? When I think about it, I'm so regretful that she died so young. But, when I remember her spirit, "to live my life as best as I can," I cannot be overwhelmed by my sorrow. Asahi, always smiling like the sun, would probably scold me. We often hear the maxim that we should live positively, but Asahi's maxim was, "We shouldn't look forward, but live in the present." She lived each moment of her life as best as she could. This is the most important aspect of life, and that spirit will give us burning passion. Now when I recall her spirit, I am truly grateful that I met her.

When I asked if I could write a book about Asahi, her mother quickly replied, "I am so glad that Asahi's life will be passed on by your words from generation to generation." During a time when she was in deep sorrow, she could not have been more receptive and cooperative, so my heart is full of thanks—more than I can express. She said, "When I talk to you about Asahi, I'm not sad at all and I feel good. Your emails are always so fun that I feel like Asahi is brought back to life. I feel like I am actually talking to Asahi and you." Her words pleased me and gave me strength, strength for me to continue to wish for Asahi to live forever. Now, I am truly grateful for Asahi's mother and Asahi's family.

Taeko Maeda

*All names but Asahi, Yūki, Ms. Mori, and Maeda are assumed ones.

BIBLIOGRAPHY

Inochi—Ichiban Taisetsuna Mono, by Mitsuo Aida (Bunka Publishing, March 2008 ©Mitsuo Aida Museum)

Shiawase wa Itsumo, by Mitsuo Aida (Bunka Publishing, March 1995 ©Mitsuo Aida Museum)

Otona no Tameno Ehon Guide—Kokoro wo Furuwasu Kando no Ehon 60, by Hideyuki Kanegaki (Softbank Creative, March 2007)

Guess How Much I Love You, by Sam McBratney and Anita Jeram, translated by Hitomi Ogawa (Hyoronsha, October 1995)

www.ingramcontent.com/pod-product-compliance
Lightning Source LLC
Chambersburg PA
CBHW022159080426
42734CB00006B/502